C000228954

# New Ideas in Indi
## Nineteenth (
## A Study of Social, Political, and
## Religious Developments

John Morrison

## Alpha Editions

This edition published in 2022

ISBN: 9789356712850

Design and Setting By

**Alpha Editions**
www.alphaedis.com

Email - info@alphaedis.com

# Contents

# PREFACE

The substance of the following volume was delivered in the form of lectures in the Universities of Glasgow and Edinburgh during Session 1904-5. As "Alexander Robertson" lecturer in the University of Glasgow, the writer dealt with the new religious ideas that have been impressing themselves upon India during the British period of her history. As "Gunning" lecturer in the University of Edinburgh, the writer dwelt more upon the new social and political ideas. The popular belief of Hindu India is, that there are no new ideas in India, that nought in India suffers change, and that as things are, so they have always been. Even educated Indians are reluctant to admit that things have changed and that their community has had to submit to education and improvement—that suttee, for example, was ever an honoured institution in the province now most advanced. But to the observant student of the Indian people, the *evolution* of India is almost as noteworthy as the more apparent rigidity. There is a flowering plant common in Northern India, and chiefly notable for the marvel of bearing flowers of different colours upon the same root. The Hindus call it "the sport of Krishna"; Mahomedans, "the flower of Abbas"; for the plant is now incorporate with both the great religions of India, and even with their far-back beginnings. Yet it is a comparatively recent importation into India; it is only the flower known in Britain as "the marvel of Peru," and cannot have been introduced into India more than three hundred years ago. It was then that the Portuguese of India and the Spaniards of Peru were first in touch within the home lands in Europe. In our own day may be seen the potato and the cauliflower from Europe establishing themselves upon the dietary of Hindus in defiance of the punctiliously orthodox. *À fortiori*—strange that we should reason thus from the trifling to the fundamental, yet not strange to the Anglo-Indian and the Indian,—*à fortiori*, we shall not be surprised to find novel and alien ideas taking root in Indian soil.

Seeds, we are told, may be transported to a new soil, either wind-borne or water-borne, carried in the stomachs of birds, or clinging by their burs to the fur of animals. In the cocoa-nut, botanists point out, the cocoa-nut palms possess a most serviceable ark wherein the seed may be floated in safety over the sea to other shores. It is thus that the cocoa-nut palm is one of the first of the larger plants to show themselves upon a new coral reef or a bare volcano-born island. Into India itself, it is declared, the cocoa-nut tree has thus come over-sea, nor is yet found growing freely much farther than seventy miles from the shore. One of the chief interests of the subject before us is that the seeds of the new ideas in India during the past century are so clearly water-borne. They are the outcome of British influence, direct or indirect.

Here are true test and evidence of the character of British influence and effort, if we can distil from modern India some of the new ideas prevailing, particularly in the new middle class. Where shall we find evidence reliable of what British influence has been? Government Reports, largely statistical, of "The Moral and Material Progress of India," are so far serviceable, but only as *crude* material from which the answer is to be distilled. Members of the Indian Civil Service, and others belonging to the British Government of India, may volunteer as expert witnesses regarding British influence, but they are interested parties; they really stand with others at the bar. The testimony of the missionary is not infrequently heard, less exactly informed, perhaps, than the Civil Servant's, but more sympathetic, and affording better testimony where personal acquaintance with the life of the people is needed. But of him too, like the Civil Servant, there is some suspicion that in one sphere he holds a brief. This, indeed, may be said in favour of the missionary's testimony, that while the Anglo-Indian identifies the missionary's standpoint with that of the native, the native identifies him with the Anglo-Indian, so that probably enough he occupies the mean of impartiality and truth. The British merchant in India may also offer as evidence, and indeed is "on the spot," and apparently qualified by reason of his independence. But the interest of his class is professedly limited to India's material progress; and of his general views, we recall what Chaucer said of the politics of his "merchant,"

"Sowninge alway th' encrees of his winning."

And finally, in increasing numbers, natives of India themselves are claiming to pronounce upon the effect of the British connection upon India; and yet again we feel that the proferred evidence must be regarded with suspicion. That Indian is exceptional indeed whose generalisations about India are based on observations and historical knowledge. If the Civil Servant's honour is bound up with a favourable verdict upon the question at issue, the educated native is as resolved upon the other side. Nay, truth requires one to say that at this time the educated Indian is virtually pledged against acknowledging any indebtedness to Britain. For the reason why, we need not anticipate, but it is foolish to shut one's eyes to the unpleasant fact, or to hide it from the British public.

Where, then, is the testimony that is reliable? Is there nothing else than the disputing, loud and long, of the six blind men of Indostan who went to *see* the Indian elephant and returned,

"Each in his own opinion
Exceeding stiff and strong,

Though each was partly in the right,
And all were in the wrong!"

From preferred testimony of all kinds, from all affidavits, however honestly sworn, we turn again to the ideas now prevailing as they *betray* themselves in the lives of the people and the words that fall from their lips. Carefully studying earlier history, we ask ourselves wherein the new ideas differ from the ideas current in India a century ago. Then as progress appears, or is absent, the forces at work stand approved or condemned. The exact historical comparison we may claim to be a special feature of this book.

The writer is not ignorant of the delicacy of the historical task he has set himself. He claims that during the twenty years he spent in India he was eager to know India and her sons, read the pamphlets and articles they wrote, enjoyed constant intercourse with Indians of all classes and religions, reckoned, as he still reckons, many Indians among his friends. He claims that during these years it was his pleasure, as well as a part of his professional duty, to study the past history of India. Ignorance of Indian history vitiates much of the writing and oratory on Indian subjects. As a member of the staff of an Indian college, with six hundred University students, the writer claims to have had exceptional opportunities of entering into the thoughts of the new middle class, and of cross-questioning upon Indian problems. In India, students "sit at the feet" of their professors, but let it not be assumed that the Oriental phrase implies a stand-off superior and crouching inferior. Nay, rather it implies the closest touch between teacher and taught. All seated tailor-fashion on the ground, the Indian teacher of former days and his disciples around him were literally as well as metaphorically in touch. The modern professor, successor of the pandit or guru, enjoys intercourse with his students, as full and free, limited in truth only by his time and his temperament.

Judging by the test of the new ideas in India, the writer has no hesitation in declaring that the British regime has been a great blessing to India. Likewise, whether directly inculcated or indirectly, some of the best features of Christian civilisation and of the Christian religion are taking hold in India and becoming naturalised. Called upon as "Alexander Robertson" lecturer in the University of Glasgow to deliver a course of lectures "in defence of the Christian faith," the writer felt that no more effective defence could be offered than this historical survey of the naturalising in India of certain distinctive features of the Christian religion and of the civilisation of western Christian lands.

Of this also the writer is sure, whether he possess the qualifications for the delicate task or lack them—there is a call for some one to interpret Britain and India to each other. In their helpless ignorance, what wonder that Britons' views are often incomplete and distorted? On the Indian side, on the other hand, the terrible anti-British feeling now prevailing in India must surely be based on ignorance and misunderstanding, and in part at least removable.

---

The Rev. Alexander Robertson, a probationer of the Free Church of Scotland, although never in office, died at Glasgow in 1879, leaving the residue of his estate for the endowment of a lectureship as aforesaid. As trustees he nominated two personal friends—the Rev. J.B. Dalgety, of the Abbey Church, Paisley, and James Lymburn, Esq., the librarian of Glasgow University. These two gentlemen made over the trust to the Glasgow University Court, and the writer had the honour of being appointed the first lecturer.

The Gunning Victoria Jubilee Lectureship in the University of Edinburgh was founded by the late Dr. R.H. Gunning of Edinburgh and Rio de Janeiro, in the year 1889. The object of the lectureship was "to promote among candidates for the ministry, and to bring out among ministers the fruits of study in Science, Philosophy, Languages, Antiquity, and Sociology."

# CHAPTER I

## THE NEW ERA—SOME LEADING WITNESSES

"The epoch ends, the world is still,
The age has talked and worked its fill;

The famous men of war have fought,
The famous speculators thought.

See on the cumbered plain,
Clearing a stage,
Scattering the past about,
Comes the New Age.
Bards make new poems;
Thinkers, new schools;
Statesmen, new systems;
Critics, new rules."

MATTHEW ARNOLD.


India is a land of manifold interest. For the visitors who crowd thither every cold season, and for the still larger number who will never see India, but have felt the glamour of the ancient land whose destiny is now so strangely linked to that of our far-off and latter-day islands, India has not one but many interests. There is the interest of the architectural glories of the Moghul emperors, in whose grand halls of audience, now deserted and merely places of show, a solitary British soldier stands sentry over a visitors' book. For the great capitals of India have moved from Delhi and Agra, the old strategic points in the centre of the great northern plain, to Calcutta, Bombay, Madras, and Rangoon, new cities on the sea, to suit the later over-sea rulers of India. There is the interest of the grand organisation of the British Government, holding in its strong paternal grasp that vast continent of three hundred million souls. Sometimes the sight of the letters V.R.I, or E.R.I. (Edwardus Rex Imperator) makes one think of the imperial S.P.Q.R.[1] once not unfamiliar in Britain. But this interest rather I would emphasise—the penetration into the remotest jungle of the great organisation of the British Government is a wonderful thing. By the coinage, the post-office, the railways, the administration of justice, the encouragement of education, the relief of famine,—by such ways the great organisation has penetrated everywhere,—in spite of faults, the greatest blessing that has come to India in her long history. Travelling by rail from Calcutta to Benares, the metropolis of Hinduism, situated upon the north bank of the sacred Ganges, we see the British rule, in symbol, in the great railway bridge spanning the river. By it old India, self-centred, exclusive, introspective, was brought into the modern world; compelled, one might say, by these great spans to admit the modern world and its conveniences, in spite of protest that the railway bridge would pollute the sacred stream. Crossing the bridge, our eyes are fixed on the outstanding feature of Benares—city of hundreds of Hindu temples. What is it? Not a Hindu temple, but a splendid Mahomedan mosque whose minarets overlook the Hindu city, calling the city of Hindus to the worship of Allah. For the site of that mosque, the Moghul emperor Aurangzeb ruthlessly cleared away a magnificent temple most sacred to the Hindus. Concerning another famous Hindu temple in the same city, listen to the Autobiography of another earlier Moghul emperor, Jahangir. "It was the belief of these people of hell [the Hindus] that a dead Hindu laid before the idol would be restored to life, if in his life he had been a worshipper there.... I employed a confidential person to ascertain the truth, and as I justly supposed, the whole was detected to be an impudent imposture.... Throwing down the temple which was the scene of this imposture, with the very same materials I erected on the spot the great mosque, because the very name of Islam was proscribed at Benares, and with God's blessing it is my desire ... to fill it full of true believers." These things I write, not to hold up to condemnation these Moghul rulers, but to point out by contrast the voluntary character of the influence during the British and Christian period. For there is in India a grander interest still than that of the British political organisation, namely, the peaceful gradual transformation of the thoughts and feelings, the hopes and fears, of each individual of the millions of India.

## The nineteenth century in India—a conflict of ideas

The real history of the past century in India has been the conflict and commingling of ideas, a Homeric struggle, renewed in the nineteenth century, between the gods of Asia and Europe. Sometimes the shock of collision has been heard, as when by Act of Legislature, in 1829, Suttee or widow-burning was put down, and, in 1891, the marriage of girls under twelve; or when by order of the Executive, the sacred privacy of Indian houses was violated in well-meant endeavours to stay the plague [1895-], great riots ensuing; or when an Indian of social standing has joined the Christian Church. At other times, like the tumbling in, unnoticed, of slice upon slice of the bank of a great Indian river flowing through an alluvial plain, opinion has silently altered, and only later observers discover that the old idea has changed. Not a hundred years ago, students of Kayasth (clerk) caste were excluded from the Sanscrit College in Calcutta. Now, without any new ordinance, they are admitted, as among the privileged castes, and the idea of the brotherhood of man has thus made way. The silent invasion is strikingly illustrated in the official *Report on Female Education in India*, 1892 to 1897. On a map of India within the *Report*, the places where female education was most advanced were coloured greener according to the degree of advance—surely most inappropriate colouring, though that is not our business. The map showed a strip of the greenest green all round the sea-coast. There the unobserved new influence came in. The *Census Report* for 1901 showed the same silently obtruding influence from over the sea in the case of the education of males. Many such silent changes might be noted. And yet again, the most diverse ideas may be observed side by side in a strange chequer. In the closing years of the nineteenth century, the University of Calcutta accepted an endowment of a lectureship "to promote Sanscrit learning and Vedantic studies," any Hindus without distinction of caste being eligible as lecturers; and then, shortly after, agreed to the request of the first lecturer that none but Hindus be admitted to the exposition of the sacred texts, thus excluding the European heads of the university from a university lecture. Perhaps the lecturer thought himself liberal, for to men like him at the beginning of the century it would have been an offence to read the sacred texts with Sudras or Hindus of humble castes. According to strict Hindu rule, only brahmans can read the sacred books.[2]

Indian ideas.

For in all three spheres, social, political, and religious, the advent of the new age implied more or less of a conflict. India has still of her own a social system, political ideas, and religious ideas and ideals. In the Indian social system, caste and the social inferiority of women stand opposed to the freedom of the individual and the equality of the sexes that prevail in Great Britain, at least in greater degree. In the sphere of politics, the absolutism, long familiar to the Indian mind, is the antithesis of the life of a citizen under a limited monarchy, with party government and unfettered political criticism. In the sphere of religion, the hereditary priesthood of India stands over against the British ideal of a clergy trained for their duties and proved in character. The Hindu conception of a religious life as a life of sacrificial offerings and penances, or of ecstasies, or of asceticism, or of sacred study, stands over against the British ideal of religion in daily life and in practical philanthropies. To the Hindu, the religious mood is that of ecstatic whole-hearted devotion; the Briton reverences as the religious mood a quiet staying intensity in noble endurance or effort.

The nineteenth century has witnessed a great transition in ideas and a great alteration in the social and political and religious standpoints. It is easy to find manifold witness to the fact from all parts of India. The biographer of the modern in ideas. Indian reformer, Malabari, a Parsee[3] writing of a Parsee, and representing Western India, is impressed by the singular fate that has destined the far-away British to affect India and her ideals so profoundly. Crossing to the east side of India, we seek a trustworthy witness. The well-known reformer, Keshub Chunder Sen, a Bengali, and representative therefore of Eastern India, declares in a lecture published in 1883: "Ever since the introduction of British power into India there has been going on a constant upheaval and development of the native mind,... whether we look at the mighty political changes which have been wrought by that ... wonderful administrative machinery which the British Government has set in motion, or whether we analyse those deep national movements of *social* and *moral* reform which are being carried on by native reformers and patriots." All Indian current opinion is unanimous with the Parsee and the Bengali that a great movement is in progress. The drift from the old moorings is a constant theme of discourse. Let Sir Alfred Lyall, once head of the United Provinces, speak for the most competent European observers. "There may be grounds for anticipating," he says, "that a solid universal peace and the impetus given by Europe must together cause such rapid intellectual expansion that India will now be carried swiftly through phases which have occupied long stages in the lifetime of other nations."[4] In another essay, in a more positive mood, he writes of British responsibility for "great non-Christian populations [in India] whose religious ideas and institutions are being rapidly transformed by English law and morality."[5] In a third passage he even prophesies rashly: "The end of simple paganism is not far distant in India."

Sir George Bird wood has also had a long Indian career, and no one suspects him of pro-British bias—rather the reverse. Yet we find him writing to the *Times* in 1895 about one of the Indian provinces, as follows: "The new Bengali language and literature," he says, "are the direct products of our Law Courts, particularly the High Court at Calcutta, of Mission schools and newspaper presses and Education Departments, the agents which are everywhere, not in Bengal only, giving if not absolute unity yet community in diversity to the peoples of British India." The modern literature of Bengal, he goes on to say, is Christian in its teaching; if not the Christianity of creed and dogma, yet of the mind of Christ.

It is that transition in ideas, that alteration in social, political, and religious standpoint which we are going to trace and illustrate.

# CHAPTER II

## INDIAN CONSERVATISM

"By the well where the bullocks go,
Silent and blind and slow."

RUDYARD KIPLING.

---

Indian conservatism.

---

Is mere inertia.

---

But while acknowledging the potent influences at work, and accepting these representative utterances, it may yet be asked by the incredulous— What of the inherent conservatism, the proverbial tenacity of India? Is there really any perceptible and significant change to record as the outcome of the influences of the nineteenth century? Well, the expression "Indian conservatism" is misleading. There is no Indian conservatism in the sense of a philosophy of politics, of society, or of religion. Indian conservatism— what is it? To some extent an idealising of the past, the golden age of great law-givers and philosophers and saints. But very much more—mere inertia and torpidity in mind and body, a reluctance to take stock of things, and an instinctive treading in the old paths. "Via trita, via tuta." In the path from one Indian village to another may often be observed an inexplicable deviation from the beeline, and then a return to the line again. It is where in some past year some dead animal or some offensive thing has fallen in the path and lain there. Year after year, long after the cause has disappeared, the feet of the villagers continue in that same deviating track. That is in perfect keeping with India. Or—to permit ourselves to follow up another natural sequence—things may quickly begin to fit in with the deviation. Perhaps the first rainy season after the feet of the villagers had been made to step aside, some plant was found in possession of the avoided spot. India-like, its right of possession was unconsciously deferred to. And then the year following, may be, one or other of the sacred fig trees appeared behind the plant, and in a few years starved it out. Ten years will make a banyan sapling, or a pipal, into a sturdy trunk, and lo, by that time, in some visitation of drought or cholera or smallpox, or because some housewife was childless, coloured threads are being tied upon the tree or some rude symbolic painting put upon it. Then an ascetic comes along and seats himself in its shade, and now, already, a sacred institution has been established that it would raise a riot to try to remove.

Visitors to Allahabad go to see the great fort erected upon the bank of the River Jumna by the Mahomedan emperor, Akbar. One of the sights of the fort, strange to tell, is the underground Hindu temple of "The Undying Banyan Tree," to which we descend by a long flight of steps. Such a sacred banyan tree as we have imagined, Akbar found growing there upon the slope of the river bank when he was requiring the ground for his fort. The undying banyan tree is now a stump or log, but it or a predecessor was visited by a Chinese pilgrim to Allahabad in the seventh century A.D. Being very tolerant, instead of cutting down the tree, Akbar built a roof over it and filled up the ground all round to the level he required. And still through the gateway of the fort and down underground, the train of pilgrims passes as of old to where the banyan tree is still declared to grow. Such is Indian conservatism, undeterred by any thought of incongruity. Benares is crowded with examples of the same unconscious tenacity. I have spoken of the ruthless levelling of Hindu temples in Benares in former days to make way for Mahomedan mosques. Near the gate of Aurangzeb's mosque a strange scene meets the eye. Where the road leads to the mosque, and with no Hindu temple nowadays in sight, are seated a number of Hindu ashes-clad ascetics. What are they doing at the entrance to a Mahomedan mosque? That is where their predecessors used to sit two hundred years ago, before Aurangzeb tore down the holy Hindu temple of Siva and erected the mosque in its stead.

> Yields before a persistent obtruding influence.

> *E.g.* British influence.

But Indian conservatism is more than an indisposition to effort and change; for the same reason, it is also an easy adaptation to things as they are found. When a new disturbing influence obtrudes from without, and persistently, it may be easier to give way than to resist. British influence is such a persistent obtrusion. In English literature as taught and read, in Christian standards of conduct, in the English language, and in the modern ideas of government and society, ever presented to the school-going section of the people of India within their own land, there is such a continuous influence from without. The impression of works like Tennyson's *In*

*Memoriam* or *Idylls of the King*, common text-books in colleges, the steady pressure of Acts of the British Government in India, like that raising the marriage age of girls; the example of men in authority like Lord Curzon, during whose vice-regal tour in South India there were no nautch entertainments; the necessity of understanding expressions like "general election" and "public spirit," and of comprehending in some measure the working of local self-government—all such constant pressure must effect a change in the mental standpoint. The army of Britain in India, representative of the imperial sceptre, has now for many years been gathered into cantonments, and its work is no longer to quell hostilities within India, but only to repel invaders from without. Other British forces, however, penetrating far deeper, working silently and for the most part unobserved, are still in the field all over India, effecting a grander change than the change of outward sovereignty. "Ideas rule the world," and he who impresses his ideas is the real ruler of men.

Indian conservatism overpowered otherwise.

Telling against Indian conservatism or inertia are other things also besides persistent Western influences. Many things Western appeal to the natural desire for advancement and comfort, and the adoption of these has often as corollary a change of idea. To take examples without further explanation. The desire for education, the key to advancement in life, has quietly ignored the old orthodox idea that education in Sanscrit and the Sacred Scriptures, *i.e.* higher education as formerly understood, is the exclusive privilege of certain castes. The very expression "higher education" has come to mean a modern English education, not as formerly an education in Sanscrit lore. Had the British Government allowed things to take their course, the still surviving institutions of the old kind for Oriental learning would have been transformed, one and all, into modern schools and colleges. Even in 1824, when Government, then under "Orientalist" influence, founded the Sanscrit College in Calcutta for the encouragement of Sanscrit learning, a numerous body of native gentlemen, with the famous Raja Rammohan Roy at their head, petitioned that a college for the study of Western learning might be established instead. For a number of years now, the Sanscrit College, then founded, has actually had fewer pupils on its rolls than it is permitted to admit at a greatly reduced fee.[6]

Again, the idea of *public questions*, the idea of the common welfare, has come into being with the nineteenth century, and is quietly repudiating caste and giving to the community a solidarity and a feeling of solidarity unknown hitherto. Upon one platform now meet, as a matter of course, the native gentlemen of all the castes, when any general grievance is felt or any great occasion falls to be celebrated. The Western custom of public meetings for the discussion of public questions is now an established Indian institution, and daily gives the lie to the idea that there is pollution in bodily contact with a person of lower caste. That a special seat should be reserved for a man because he is a brahman would be scouted. The convenience of travelling by rail or in tram-cars has been even more widely effective in dissolving the idea. And if the advantage or convenience of the new ways can overcome the force of custom, so can the unprofitableness of the old. For illustrations, I pass from the gentlemen who attend public meetings where the speeches are in English, to the less educated and more superstitious and more blindly conservative people. In the Mahratta districts of the Central Provinces, says the *Census Report* for 1901, in recent years an unavoidable scepticism as to his efficiency has tended to reduce the earnings of the Garpagari or averter of hail from the crops. In Calcutta the same influence has extinguished the trade of supplier of Ganges water. The water taps in the house or on the street are too convenient, and the quality of the water is too manifestly superior for the desecration from the iron pipes to outweigh the advantages. A few years ago, in Darjeeling, north of Bengal, the brahman names upon the signs of the liquor shops were distinctly in the majority. The sacerdotal caste, new style, had appreciated the chances of big profits and shut their eyes to the regulations of caste, which have relegated drink-sellers to a very low place in the scale. Brahmans are even said to figure among the contractors who supply beef, flesh of the sacred animal, to the British army in India. "A curious sign of the changing time," says Mr. Lockwood Kipling (*Beast and Man in India*), "is the fact that Hindus of good caste, seeing the profit that may be made from leather, are quietly creeping into a business from which they are levitically barred. Money prevails against caste more potently than missionary preaching."

In this region, where convenience or comfort or personal advancement are concerned, it may safely be asserted that the so-called Indian conservatism has not much resisting power. There, at least, it is found that where there is a will there is a way.[7]

---
The Indian mind awakened.
---

And there is a higher influence at work dissolving and reconstituting the whole framework of ideas. Upon the Indian mind, long lain fallow, modern civilisation and modern thought and the fellowship with the world are acting as the quickening rain and sunshine upon the fertile Indian soil. That these and similar obtruding influences have had a transforming effect has already been alleged. But far beyond, in promise at least, is the revived activity of the Indian mind itself. If the age of Elizabeth be the outcome of the stirring of the minds of Englishmen through the discovery of a new world, the multiplication of books, the revival of learning, and the reformation of religion, how shall we measure the effect upon the acute Indian mind of the far more stimulating influences of this Indian Renaissance! What comparison, for example, can be made between the stimulus of the new learning of the sixteenth century and the stimulus of the first introduction to a modern library? It would be an exaggeration to say that the Indian mind is now showing all its power in response to the stimulus. But it is everywhere active, and in some spheres, as in Religion and Philanthropy, in History, in Archæology, in Law, in certain Natural Sciences, individuals have already done service to India and contributed to knowledge. Glimpses of great regions, unexplored, in these domains are rousing students to secure for themselves a province. "More copies of books of poetry, philosophy, law, and religion now issue every year from the press of British India than during any century of native rule."[8] Of course it would be misleading to ignore the fact that reaction as well as progress has its apostles among the awakened minds of India. Much of the awakened mental activity, also, is spent—much wasted—on political writing and discussion, which is often uninformed by knowledge of present facts and of Indian history. The general poverty also, and the so-called Western desire to "get on," prevent many from becoming in any real sense students or thinkers or men of public spirit.

Indian conservatism, therefore, we contend, is not the insurmountable obstacle to new ideas that many superficially deem it to be.

# CHAPTER III

## NEW SOCIAL IDEAS

*[Purusha, the One Spirit, embodied,]*

"Whom gods and holy men made their oblation.
With Purusha as victim, they performed
A sacrifice. When they divided him,
How did they cut him up? What was his mouth?
What were his arms? And what, his thighs and feet?
The Brahman was his mouth; the kingly soldier
Was made his arms; the husbandman, his thighs;
The servile Sudra issued from his feet."

From the *Rigveda*, Mandala x. 90,
translated by Sir M. MONIER WILLIAMS.

---
  Caste represses individuality.
---

New ideas in the social sphere first claim our attention. The individual and the community, each have rights, says a writer on the philosophy of history, and it is hurtful when the balance is not preserved. If the community be not securely established, the individuals will have no opportunity to develop; if the individual be not free, the community can have no real greatness. Speaking broadly, when Western social ideas meet Indian, the conflict is between the rights of the individual as in Western civilisation, and the rights of the community or society as in the Indian. India stands for the statical *social* forces, modern Europe for the dynamical and *individualistic*. In India, as in France before the Revolution, certain established usages are prejudicially affecting the progress of the individual, fettering him in many ways. I refer to caste, the denial of the brotherhood of mankind, the artificial barricading of class from class, the sacrifice of the individual to his class—condemned by native reformers like Ramananda, Kabir, Nanak, and Chaitanya long before the advent of European ideas. Whatever the origin or original advantages of the caste system, it has long operated to repress individuality.[9] It is a vast boycotting agency ready to hand to crush social non-conformity.[10] One can easily understand that if society is rigidly organised for certain social necessities (marriage for example) into a number of mutually exclusive sets or circles, admission to all of which is by birth only, an individual cast out from any set must perish. No one will eat with him, no one will intermarry with him or his sons and daughters. It is into such a society that modern social ideas have been sown, the ideas let us say of John Stuart Mill's book, *On Liberty*—the *individual's* liberty, that is to say—which used to be a common university text-book in India.

> Caste suggests an imperfect idea of the community.

> Nevertheless, a practical solidarity in Hinduism.

Besides setting the community too much above the individual, the caste system is faulty in presenting to the Indian mind an imperfect idea of the community. The caste is the natural limit to one's interest and consciousness of fellowship, to the exclusion of the larger community. According to Raja Rammohan Roy, writing in 1824, the caste divisions are "*as* destructive of national union as of social enjoyment." In *Modern India*, Sir Monier Williams expresses himself similarly. Caste "tends to split up the social fabric into numerous independent communities, and to prevent all national and patriotic combinations." Too much, however, may be made of this, for the practical solidarity of Hinduism, in spite of caste divisions, is one of the most striking of social phenomena in India. Whatever may have brought it about, the solidarity of Hinduism is an undeniable fact. The supremacy of the priestly caste over all may have been a bond of union, *as* likewise the necessity of all castes to employ the priests, for the Jewish ritual and the tribe of Levi were the bonds of union among the twelve tribes of Israel. Sir Alfred Lyall virtually defines Hinduism as *the employment of brahman priests*, and it is the adoption of brahmans as celebrants in social and religious ceremonies that marks the passing over of a non-Hindu community into Hinduism. It is thus it becomes a new Hindu caste.[11] Then, uniting further the mutually exclusive castes, many are the common heritages, actual or adopted, of traditions and sacred books, and the common national epics of the Ramayan and the Mahabharat. The cause of the solidarity is not a common creed, as we shall see when we reach the consideration of new religious ideas, ideas.

> New ideas opposed to caste, namely, individual liberty and nationality.

If Hinduism as a social system is to be moved by the modern spirit, we may look for movement in the direction of freedom of individual action, that is, the loosening of caste; we may look for larger ideas of nationality and citizenship, superseding to some extent the idea of caste. As is not infrequent in India, Government pointed out the way for public opinion. In 1831 the Governor-General, Lord William Bentinck, issued his fiat that no native be debarred from office on account of caste, creed, or race, and that a son who had left his father's religion did not thereby forfeit his inheritance.

---
### Loosening of caste.
---

To any observer it is now plain that while caste is still a very powerful force, and even while new castes, new social rings, are being formed through the working of the spirit of exclusiveness, the general ideas of caste are undergoing change. In these latter days one can hardly credit the account given of the consternation in Calcutta in 1775, when the equality of men before the law was asserted, and the *brahman*, Nanda-kumar, was hanged for forgery. Many of the orthodox brahmans shook off the dust of the polluted city from their feet and quitted Calcutta for a new residence across the Hooghly. In 1904, we find conservative Hindus only writing to the newspapers to complain that even in the Hindu College at Benares, the metropolis of Hinduism, some of the members of the College Committee were openly violating the rules of caste. In the same year a Calcutta Hindu newspaper, the *Amrita Bāzār Patrikā*, declared, "Caste is losing its hold on the Hindu mind."[12] The recent denunciation of caste by an enlightened Hindu ruler, the Gaekwar of Baroda, is a further significant sign of the times.

---
### Offences against caste.
---

What does caste forbid and punish? Freedom of thought, if not translated into social act, has not been an offence against caste at any time in the period under review, neither has caste taken cognisance of sins against morality as such. The sins that caste has punished have been chiefly five, as follows: Eating forbidden food, eating with persons of lower caste, crossing the sea, desertion of Hinduism for another religion, marrying with a person of a lower caste, and, in many communities also, marrying a widow. The Hindustani proverb, "Eight brahmans, nine cooking-places," hits off with a spice of *proverbial* exaggeration the old punctiliousness about food. The sin of eating forbidden food is thus described by Raja Rammohan Roy in 1816: "The chief part of the theory and practice of Hinduism, I am sorry to say," writes the Raja, "is made to consist in the adoption of a peculiar mode of diet; the least aberration from which (even though the conduct of the offender may in other respects be pure and blameless) is not only visited with the severest censure, but actually punished by exclusion from the society of his family and friends. In a word, he is doomed to undergo what is commonly called loss of caste."[13] Now, in respect of the first three of these offences, in all large centres of population the general attitude is rapidly changing. In the light of modern ideas, these prohibitions of certain food and of certain company at food, and of sea voyages, are fading like ghosts at dawn. An actual incident of a few years ago reveals the prevailing conflict of opinion, especially with regard to the serfdom which ties down Indians to India.

An actual case.

Two scions of a leading family in a certain provincial town of Bengal, brave heretics, made a voyage to Britain and the Continent, and while away from home, it was believed, flung caste restrictions to the winds. On their return, the head of the family gave a feast to all of the caste in the district, and no one objected to the presence of the two voyagers at the feast. This was virtually their re-admission into caste. But shortly after, a document was circulated among the caste complaining, without naming names, of the readmission of such offenders. The tactics employed by the family of the offenders are noteworthy. The demon of caste had raised his head, and they dared not openly defy him. So the defence set up was the marvellous one that, while on board ship and in Europe, the young men had never eaten any forbidden or polluted food. They had lived upon fruit, it was said, which no hand except their own had cut. The old caste sentiment was so strong that the family of the voyagers felt compelled to bring an action for libel against the publishers of the circular. They lost their case, as no offender had been mentioned by name, and the tyranny of caste thus indirectly received the support of the courts.

Of course it would still be easier to discover instances of the tyranny of caste than the assertion of liberty, even among highly educated men. In this matter of emancipation also, North India is far ahead of the South. While minister at the court of Indore, 1872-75, the late Sir T. Madhava Rao, a native of South India, was invited to go to England to give evidence on Indian Finance before a Committee of the House of Commons. *On religious grounds* he was not able to accept the invitation.[14] Nor is it generally known that the Bengali nobleman who represented his country at the King's coronation in London belongs to a family that is out of caste. If the newspapers are to be believed, an orthodox Bengali Hindu was first invited to attend the coronation, and was "unable to accept." Had that gentleman accepted and gone, his example might at once have emancipated his countrymen. But he did not know his hour. "There is a venial as well as a damning sin," we may note, in regard to this crossing of the sea. "A man may cross the Indian Ocean to Africa and still remain an orthodox Hindu. The sanctity of caste is not affected. But let him go to Europe, and his caste as well as his creed is lost in the sea."[15] An orthodox Hindu has never been seen in Britain.

It is worth noting also, that in earlier times it involved loss of caste to go away South, even within India itself, among the Dravidean peoples beyond the known Aryan pale in the North. Thus, slowly the cords of serfdom lengthen.

Towards the fourth of the offences against caste, namely, the adoption of a new religion, the general attitude has likewise changed, although to a less degree. In large towns, at least, the convert to Christianity is not so rigidly or so instantaneously excluded from society as he used to be, and the Indian Christian community, although small, is now in many places one of the recognised sections of the community.

This certainly may be asserted, that the modern Hindus are being familiarised as never before with non-brahman leaders, religious and social. Neither of the recent Brāhma (Theistic) leaders, the late Keshub Chunder Sen and the late Protap Chunder Mozumdar, was brahman by caste. The great Bombay reformer, the Parsee, Malabari, is not even a Hindu. The founder of the Arya sect, the late Dyanand Saraswati, was out of caste altogether, being the son of a brahman father and a low-caste mother. The late Swami Vivekananda (Narendranath *Dutt*, B.A.), who represented Hinduism at the Parliament of Religions in Chicago in 1893, was not a brahman, as his real surname plainly declares. While, most wonderful of all, the accepted leaders of the pro-Hindu Theosophists, champions of Hinduism more Hindu than the Hindus, after whom the educated Hindus flock, are not even Indians; alas, they belong, the most prominent of them, to the inferior female sex! I mean the Russian lady, the late Madame Blavatsky, the English ladies Mrs. Annie Besant and Miss Noble [Sister Nivedita], and the American, Colonel Olcott. Which side of that glaring incongruity is to give way—brahman and caste ideas, or the buttressing of caste ideas by outcastes, Feringees, like Mrs. Besant? It would be interesting to hear an orthodox brahman upon Mrs. Besant's claim to have had a previous Hindu existence as a Sanscrit pandit. What sin did the pandit commit, would be his natural reflection, that he was born again a Feringee, and a woman?

Unpardonable offences.

But the offence of the fifth sin, marrying below one's caste, or the marriage of widows, seems as rank as ever. Upon these points, rather, the force of caste seems concentrating. The marriage of widows will be considered when we come to discuss the social inferiority of woman in India. To marry within one's caste promises to be the most persistent of all the caste ideas. The official observation is that "whatever may have been the origin and the earlier developments of caste, this prohibition of mixed marriages stands forth now as its essential and most prominent characteristic. The feeling against such unions is deeply engrained." And again, a second pronouncement on caste: "The regulations regarding food and drink are comparatively fluid and transitory, while those relating to marriage are remarkably stable and absolute."[16] The pro-Hindu lady, already referred to, also agrees. "Of hereditary caste," she says, "the essential characteristic is the refusal of intermarriage."[17] Even Indian Christians are reluctant to marry below their old caste, and value a matrimonial alliance with a higher. To that residuum of caste, when it becomes the residuum, one could not object. The Aryan purity of the stock may be a fiction, as authorities declare it to be in the great majority of castes and in by far the greater part of India; but given the belief in the purity of blood, the desire to preserve it is a natural desire. If one may prophesy, then, regarding the fate of the caste system under the prevailing modern influences, castes will survive longest simply as a number of in-marrying social groups. To that hard core the caste idea is being visibly worn down.

Support of caste by British authorities.

With strange obliviousness surely, the British officials are lending support to caste ideas in various ways, while many of the best minds in India are groaning under the tyranny. The compilers of the *Report of the Census of India for* 1901, gentlemen to whom every student of India is deeply indebted, in their enumeration of castes, give the imprimatur of government to such Cimmerian notions as that the touch of certain low castes is defiling to the higher. The writer and condoner of the following paragraph surely need a lengthy furlough to Britain or the States. We read that "the table of social precedence attached to the *Cochin Report* shows that while a Nayar can pollute a man of a higher caste only by touching him, people of the Kammalan group, including masons, blacksmiths, carpenters, and workers in leather, pollute at a distance of 24 feet, toddy drawers at 36 feet, Palayan or Cheruman cultivators at 48 feet; while in the case of the Paraiyan (Pariahs) who eat beef, the range of pollution is stated to be no less than 64 feet." Some consolation let us even here take from the fact that in an earlier publication the extreme range of the polluting X-rays of the pariah is stated to be 72 feet. So there has been 8 feet of progress for the pariah. But our point is, that interesting as all that table of precedence no doubt is, it is out of place in a Government report, which may be quoted against a poor low-caste man as authoritative pronouncement regarding his social position. Justice and humanity, good grounds in the eyes of the Indian Government ere now for legislating contrary to caste ideas, ought to have enjoined the ignoring of caste ideas here. It is no mere fancy that after an accident one of these low-caste masons in South India might be brought to the door of a Government hospital and be refused admission by a native medical officer because his presence polluted at a distance of 24 feet—has not the Government Report declared it so? It is no fancy, for a year or two ago the Post Office reported that in one village the Post Office was found located where low castes were not allowed to approach. In some provinces, also, teachers will object to the admission of low-caste children in their schools; or "if they admit them make them sit outside in the verandah."[18] What now of the dignity of manual labour which many a high official has expounded to native youth? Or to take another instance of un-British countenancing of the caste idea. The Shahas of *Bengal* are a humble caste, and the members of higher castes will not, as a rule, take water at their hands, so the Government Report tells us. On the other hand, the Shahas of *Assam*, immigrants from Bengal, have managed to raise themselves high in the social scale. Why, when an Assam Shaha takes up his residence again in his motherland, Bengal, should this Blue-book be casting up to him his humble origin? Why this un-British weighting of those who are behind in the race? Again, at the very time of the Census, the Maratha caste was in conflict with the brahman in two Native States of Western India, Kohlapur and Baroda, over a matter of religious privileges. The brahman contention is that the Mahratta pretensions to high-caste blood [kshatriya] are groundless, and now we have the very same statement in the *Census Report*, backing "the king of the castle" against "the dirty rascal." Not a century ago, students of kayasth [clerk] caste were excluded from the Sanscrit College in Calcutta; they are now within the privileged circle, but their claim might not yet have been made good had a Government Blue-book of these earlier days been allowed to brand them as debarred from the College by their caste. At a public meeting the writer heard one of the most learned and respected Hindus of Calcutta respectfully protest to the Lieutenant-Governor against the public recognition in the *Census Report* of such irrational social grading.[19]

Similarly in the provision by Government of Caste Hostels for students. According to the first rule of the Hindu Hostel in connection with the Government College in Calcutta, "none but respectable Hindu students ... shall be admitted,... and such inmates shall observe the rules and usages of Hindu Society." In that rule, "respectable" simply means *other than low caste*. Now for the *reductio ad absurdum*. A certain Bengali gentleman of low caste was some years ago entitled to be addressed as "Honourable," from the high public office he held, yet by departmental orders the Principal of the Government College would shut the door of the College Hostel in the face of the Honourable's son.

New religious organisations repudiate caste.

Of the new religious organisations of educated India, three repudiate caste, namely, the Protestant Christian community, the Brāhma Samāj or Theistic Association, chiefly found in Bengal, and the Ārya Samāj or Vedic Association of the United Provinces and the Punjab. These forces of new religious feeling are marshalled against caste as a social anomaly and a bar to progress. Mahomedanism in its day was a powerful force arrayed against caste, but its regenerating power has long ago evaporated, for in many districts of India caste ideas are found flourishing among the Mahomedan converts from Hinduism. They have carried over the caste ideas from their old to their new religion.[20] The Sikhs in the Punjab also repudiate caste, but they too have forgotten their old reforming mission. Notwithstanding, we repeat, Northern India owes an immense debt to these two religions, particularly to Mahomedanism. Let any one who doubts it observe the caste thraldom of Southern India, where Mahomedan rule never established itself. Irrational as caste is in Northern India, it is tenfold more so in the South, as we have already seen. A noteworthy assertion of "the rights of men," or more literally of the rights of women, against caste may be noted in that same caste-bound South India. In the Native State of Travancore, caste custom had prohibited the women of the lower castes from wearing clothing above the waist. But about the year 1827, the women who became Christians began to don a loose jacket as the women of higher caste had been in the habit of doing. Bitter persecution of the Christian women followed, but in 1859 the right of these lower-caste women to wear an upper cloth was legally acknowledged.[21]

But the outstanding evidence of new ideas in regard to caste is furnished by the Hindu revivalists who, under the leading of Mrs. Annie Besant and the Theosophists, have established the Hindu College, Benares, as a buttress of Hinduism. From the *Text-book of Hindu Religion* prepared for the College, we learn that these representatives and champions of orthodoxy defend caste only to the extent of the ancient fourfold division of society into brahmans, rulers, merchants and agriculturists (one caste), and servants. What, we may ask, is to become of the 1886 sub-divisions of the brahman caste alone, all mutually exclusive with regard to inter-marriage? The text-book actually quotes sacred texts to show that caste depends on conduct, not on birth, and refers to bygone cases of promotion of heroes to a higher caste without rebirth. Its final pronouncement on caste is that "unless the abuses that are interwoven with it can be eliminated, its doom is certain." So far has the opinion of orthodox conservative Hinduism progressed with reference to its fundamental social feature, caste.

# CHAPTER IV

## THE CHIEF SOLVENT OF THE OLD IDEAS

"Let knowledge grow from more to more,
But more of reverence in us dwell;
That mind and soul according well,
May make one music as before."

TENNYSON, *In Memoriam.*

---

English education the chief solvent.

---

English education is the chief solvent of old ideas in India and the chief source from which the new are supplied. English is the language of the freest peoples in the world. It is only to be expected, therefore, that with the spread of English education in India the idea of individual freedom and the feeling of nationality should grow and the caste idea decline. The beginning of the process is often witnessed among the boys in Secondary Schools in India. You lay your hand upon the arm of a boy, a new-comer to the school, and you ask him in English, "What class?" He answers "Brahman," giving you his caste instead of his class in school. The boy will not be long in the English school before he will classify himself differently. In a dozen ways each day he is made to feel that the school and the modern world have another standard for boys and men than the caste. Or take another example of the educative effect of a study of English—I can vouch for its genuineness. In your house in India you get into friendly conversation with a half-educated shopkeeper or native tradesman. You ask in English how many children he has, and his reply is, "I have not any children, I have three daughters." Just a little more reading in English literature would have taught him that elsewhere the daughter is a child of the family equally with the son.

There, in these two examples, the great social problems of India present themselves—caste and the social inferiority of women, and in the English language we see India confronted with ideas different from her own. Take a third illustration from the socio-religious sphere. Few Hindus think of Hinduism as a system of religious practices and doctrines to be justified by reason or by spiritual intuition, or by the spiritual satisfaction it can afford to mankind. No, Hinduism is a thing for Indians, and belongs to the Indian soil. The converse of the idea is that Christianity is a foreign thing, the religion of the intruding ruling race. It is not for Indians. A vigorous patriotic pamphlet, published in 1903, entitled *The Future of India*, assumes plainly that *Hindus* and *Indians* mean the same thing. The pamphlet speaks of the relations of Indians to "other races, such as Mahomedans, Parsees, and Christians," as if these were less truly Indians than the Hindus. To the writer, manifestly, Hinduism is a racial thing. To him, however, or to the next generation after him, further study of modern history will make clear that only in a slight degree and a few instances is religion a racial thing, and that there are laws and a science of spiritual as of bodily health. Once more, how ill-fitting are, say, the Indian word *mukti* (deliverance from further lives, the end of transmigrations) and the English word *salvation*, although *mukti* and *salvation* are often regarded as equivalents.

To the man instructed in English, such contrasts are always being presented, tacitly inviting him to compare and to modify. We can put ourselves in the place of many a youth of sixteen or seventeen, hope of the village school, going up to enter a college in one of the larger towns of India. He is entering the new world. Should he be of brahman caste, it may profit him a little, for he will still meet with many non-brahman householders ready to find him in food and lodging simply because he is a poor brahman student. Of course he is looking forward to one of the new professions, Law, or Medicine, or Engineering, or Teaching, or Government Service. In *these* it is patent to him that caste is of no account. High caste or low, he and all his fellow-students are aware they must prove themselves and fight their way up. The leading place at the bar is no more a high-caste man's privilege than it is his privilege to be exempted from standing in the dock or suffering the extreme penalty of the law. We have already referred to the effect of the assertion of the equality of men before the law in 1775 in the hanging of the brahman, Nandakumar, for forgery. Now, looking back at the dissolving of the old ideas of artificial rank and privileges, we may reckon also the equality of men in the great modern professions, foremost in India being Law, as among the chief dissolving agencies.

> Extent of English education.

> English words naturalised.

It is easy to give *figures* at least for the vast agency now at work in the spread of English education in India. Higher English education for natives began with the founding of the Hindu College in Calcutta in 1817; in the year 1902 there were in India five Universities, the examinations of which are conducted in English; and affiliated to these examining Universities were 188 teaching colleges containing 23,009 undergraduates; and preparing for the Matriculation Examination (in the year 1896-97) were 5267 Secondary Schools, containing 535,155 pupils. From these Secondary Schools in the year 1901, 21,750 candidates appeared at the Matriculation Examinations of the Universities professing to be able to write their answers in English, and of these nearly 8000 passed. That figure is a measure of the process of leavening India with modern ideas through English education—8000 fresh recruits a year. That is the measure of the confusion introduced into the old social organism. A small number, no doubt, compared with the ten million of unleavened youth born in the same year, and yet they are the pick of the middle classes and must become the leaders of the masses. The masses in China, it is alleged, would not be anti-foreign were it not for the influence of their literati, and the thoughts of these Indian literati must also become the thoughts of the Indian masses. It is the mind of these literati, mainly, which we are trying to gauge. According to the census of 1901 their total number approached one million, being those who could read and write English. Descending below the English-reading literati, I have noted about three hundred English words naturalised in two of the chief vernaculars of India, an indication, if not a measure, of the new influence among the masses.

Too sanguine prophecies of progress.

Yet having tabulated figures, once more, ere we proceed, we enjoin upon ourselves and our readers a cautious estimate of the progress of ideas. The European hood and gown of the Indian student may merely *drape* an *unchanged* being. Writing in 1823 about the encouragement of education and the teaching of English and the translation of English books, the Governor of Bombay, Mountstuart Elphinstone, declared too confidently that "the conversion of the natives *must* result from the diffusion of knowledge among them." Macaulay, similarly, writing from India in 1836 to his father, the well-known philanthropist, declares: "It is my firm belief that if our plans of[English] education are followed up, there will not be a single idolater among the respectable classes in Bengal thirty years hence." Omar Khayyam's words suggest themselves as the other extreme of opinion regarding English education in India, inside of which the truth will be found:

"Myself when young did eagerly frequent
Doctor and saint, and heard great argument

About it and about, but evermore
Came out by that same door wherein I went."

The lines express the view of many Anglo-Indians. We may reply that anywhere only a few individuals are positively liberalised by a liberal education. We must patiently wait while their standpoint becomes the lore and tradition of the community.

-------------------------------------------------------------------------
Reformers are English-speaking; reactionaries are ignorant of English.
-------------------------------------------------------------------------

The part played by English education in the introduction of new ideas is apparent whenever we enumerate the leading reformers of the nineteenth century. One and all have received a modern English education, and several of them have made some name by addresses and publications in English. Of Indian reformers, distinguished also as English scholars, may be named with all honour:

1. Rammohan Roy, a great opponent of Suttee and Idolatry, who also dared to make the voyage to England. He died at Bristol in 1833.

2. Iswar Chunder Vidyasagar, a great upholder of the right of widows to remarry and an advocate of education, both elementary and higher. He died at Calcutta in 1891.

3. K.M. Banerjea, D.L., C.I.E., an opponent of the caste system, the greatest scholar among Indian Christians. He died at Calcutta in 1885.

4. Keshub Chunder Sen, religious reformer, an advocate of a higher marriage age for girls. He died at Calcutta in 1884.

5. Mr. Behramji Malabari, an advocate of a higher marriage age for girls—of the Bombay side of India.

6. The late Mr. Justice M.G. Ranade, a social reformer of Bombay.

7. The late Mr. Justice K.T. Telang, C.I.E., an opponent of child marriages and a social reformer of Bombay.

8. The late Raja Sir T. Madhava Rao, K.C.S.I., a social reformer, of the Madras Presidency—died in 1891.

Pandita Ramabhai, it may be noted, had entered upon her career as a champion of female education before she began the study of English.

-------------------------------------------------------------------------
Sanguine estimate of progress.
-------------------------------------------------------------------------

In striking contrast with all these in this respect are the men who represent the extreme conservative or reactionary spirit, who as a rule are as ignorant of English as the great reformers are the reverse. We may cite, in illustration:

1. Dyanand Saraswati, founder of the new sect of Āryas in the United Provinces and Punjab. Their chief doctrine, the infallibility of the Vedas or earliest Hindu scriptures, is reactionary, although a number of reforms are inculcated in the name of a return to the Vedas.

2. The late Ramkrishna Paramhansa, a famous Bengali ascetic of high spiritual tone, but of the old type.

3. The gentleman already referred to, who as University lecturer on Hindu Philosophy in Calcutta insisted that none but Hindus be admitted to the exposition of the sacred texts, shutting out the Chancellor, the Vice-Chancellor, and many Fellows of the University.

4. Sanscrit pundits, very conservative as a class, and generally unfamiliar with English.

New Hinduism in contact with the modern educational influences was most interestingly manifest in the person of Swami Vivekananda (*Reverend Rational-bliss* we may render his adopted name), representative of Hinduism at the Parliament of Religions in Chicago in 1893. The representative Hindu was not even a member of the priestly caste, as we have already told. It were tedious to analyse his Hinduism, as set forth at Chicago and elsewhere, into what was Christianity or modern thought, and what, on the other hand, was Hinduism. Suffice it to say that as Narendra Nath Dutt, B.A., he figures on the roll of graduates of the Church of Scotland's College in Calcutta. While a student there, he sat at the feet of two teachers representing the new and the old, the West and the East. In the College classroom he received religious instruction from Dr. Hastie, the distinguished theologian who afterwards taught Scottish students of theology in the University of Glasgow. At the same time he was in the habit of visiting the famous Bengali ascetic, Ramkrishna Paramhansa, already mentioned, and of communing with him. Returning from Chicago crowned with the honour which his earnestness, his eloquence, his power of reasoning, his attractive manner, and his striking physique and dress called forth, Young India lionised him; Old India met in Calcutta and resolved that Mr. Dutt of kayasth caste must drop the brahman title *Swami*, which he had assumed, before *they* could recognise him. In 1895, having gone to Dakhineswar, the old residence of his Hindu master, Ramkrishna, Swami Vivekananda was actually expelled from the temple where his master had been wont to worship. The Chicago representative of Hinduism had been guilty of the sins of crossing the sea and of living like a European, and so he must be disowned and the temple purged of his presence. After a few years, Swami Vivekananda bravely settled down to unobtrusive, philanthropic work, one had almost said *Christian philanthropic work*, in a suburb of Calcutta, denouncing caste and idolatry and the outcasting of those who had crossed the sea, and recommending the Hindus to take to flesh-eating. There, and while so engaged, in 1902 he died. How shall we ticket that strange personage? Kayasth caste as he was born, or new brahman? Swami or B.A. of a Mission College of the modern Calcutta University? A conservative or a reformer? Hindu ascetic or Christian philanthropist? He stands for India in transition, old and new ideas commingling. He is a typical product of the English and Christian education given to multitudes in India to-day.

# CHAPTER V

## WOMAN'S PLACE

"To lift the woman's fallen divinity
Upon an equal pedestal with man's."

"The woman's cause is man's; they rise or sink
Together, dwarfed or godlike, bond or free."

TENNYSON, *The Princess.*

---
Social inferiority of women.
---

Next to caste, the chief social feature of India is the position of women in the community. Hindus and Mahomedans alike assign to the female sex an inferior position. In Mahomedan mosques, for example, no woman is ever seen at prayer; she would not be permitted to take part. Only by the neglect of female children in India, and the special disadvantages from which women suffer there, can it be explained why in India in 1901 there were only 963 females to every 1000 males. In India, as in Europe and all the world over, more boys than girls are born, but in the course of life the balance is soon redressed, and in the whole population in every country in Europe, except Italy[22] and Bulgaria, the females actually outnumber the males. Why are the Indian figures so different? Pro-Hindu enthusiasts may glorify the Hindu social system, and wish to deny the social inferiority of the female sex; average Anglo-Indians may be suspected of being unsympathetic in their statements; but the Census figures stand, and demand an explanation. Where are these 37 girls and women out of every 1000—over five million altogether? Common humanity demands an answer of India, for we seem to hear a bitter cry of India's womanhood. As infants, less cared for; as girls, less educated; married too early; ignorantly tended in their hour; as married ladies, shut out of the world; always more victimised by ignorance and superstition—in life's race, India's women carry a heavy handicap, and 37 out of every 1000 actually succumb.

In the matter of the social elevation of their sex, it appears to the writer that Anglo-Indian ladies fall far short of what they might do. A fair number do interest themselves in their Indian sisters through the lady missionaries and lady doctors, but first-hand knowledge of the lives of Indian women is very rare indeed. Our late revered Queen's interest in India and in the womanhood of India is well known, but her feeling about the duty of Anglo-Indian ladies I have never seen recorded. Speaking at Balmoral to an Indian Christian lady, a member of one of the royal families of India—the only lady perhaps who ever conversed in Hindustani with Queen Victoria—she expressed her regret that more Anglo-Indian ladies did not get up the native language, sufficiently at least to let them visit their Indian sisters. Than Christian sisterly sympathy thus expressed, what better link also could there be between two communities which many things seem to be forcing apart?

---

Suttee and female infanticide.

---

It would be unjust to depreciate the influence of mother and wife among Hindus, and we freely acknowledge that, after custom, the mainstay of the zenana system is concern for the purity of the female members of the household. Saying that, we must now also note that modern ideas of the just rights of the female sex have made little progress in India. Some progress there has been, judging by the standard already applied; for although in 1901 there were only 963 females to every 1000 males, in the year 1891 there were only 958, and in the year 1881 still fewer, namely, 954. But it seems as if in India we had justification of the law of social progress that woman's rights will not be recognised until man's have been. The brotherhood of man must be established before men recognise that sister women too have rights. Translating into Indian terms, and without professing to have given positive proof—caste feeling must still further decay before the position of women becomes much improved. At all events, judging by the past, it almost seems to have been necessary for the Legislature to intervene to secure any progress for the sex and give a foothold to the new ideas, glaringly unfair to the sex as the old ideas were. Thus in 1870 female infanticide, earlier prohibited in single provinces, was put down by law throughout India; although there are localities still in which the small proportion of female children justifies the belief that female infanticide is not extinct.[23] Nevertheless, let the progress of the new ideas regarding women be noted; we compare the hesitating *inference* of the practice of female infanticide in the *Indian Census Report* of 1901 with the voluminous evidence in the two volumes of Parliamentary Papers on Infanticide in India published in 1824 and 1828. Kathiawar and Cutch, Baroda and Rajputana, round Benares and parts of Oude and Madras were the localities particularly infected with the barbarous custom in the first quarter of the century. But to return to the recognition of the rights of women in legislative enactments. In 1829 an Act of the Supreme

- 30 -

Government in Bengal made Suttee or the burning of a widow upon the dead husband's pyre an offence for all concerned. In 1830 similar Acts were passed by the Governments of Madras and Bombay, and the abolition of Suttee is now universally approved.[24] Such is the educative influence of a good law. Perhaps a would-be patriot may yet occasionally be heard so belauding the devotion of the widows who burned themselves that his praise is tantamount to a lament over the abolition of Suttee. But the general sentiment has been completely changed since the first quarter of the nineteenth century, when the Missionaries and some outstanding Indians like the Bengali reformer Rammohan Roy agitated for the abolition of Suttee, and the Government, convinced, still hesitated to put down a custom so generally approved. In these changed times it will hardly be believed that Rammohan Roy only ventured to argue against any form of compulsion being put upon the widow, and that the orthodox champions of the practice appealed against the abolition not only to the Governor-General, but also to the King in Council,—the petition having been heard in the House of Lords in 1832. But once more to return to the emancipation of women by Acts of the Legislature. By another Act, in 1856, the Indian Government abolished the legal restrictions to widow marriage. Still another Act, in 1891, forbade cohabitation before the age of twelve; and although fiercely opposed in the native press and in mass meetings, the Act, which expressed the views of many educated Hindus, is now apparently acquiesced in by all, and must be educating the community into a new idea of marriage.

In five aspects the social inferiority of the female sex is still apparent— namely, in the illiteracy of females, in marriage before womanhood, in polygamy, in the seclusion of women, and in the prohibition of the marriage of widows. Excepting the last, no one of these customs is imposed by caste, nor is the last even in every caste.

Their lack of education.

The inferior position still assigned to women in Indian society can best be shown in figures. The indifference to their education is manifest when for all India, rich and poor, European and native, in 1901, there were fourteen times as many men as women who could read and write. Only one female in 144 was educated to that extent, and the movement for female education has practically been at a stand-still for some years, in spite of the increase of native Christians, Brahmas, and Āryas, who all advocate the education of girls, and in spite of fostering by Governments and missionaries. Taking *British* India by itself, there was a higher proportion of educated females, as we should of course expect, although that only makes the proportion less elsewhere. In British India, about 1 in 100 [9 per 1000] could read and write; but even there, less than 1 per cent. The quickening of ideas in cities is apparent. In the cities there are proportionally more than twice as many educated females as in the whole country.

---

: Premature marriage.

---

The injustice done to the sex by marriage before womanhood is apparent from another paragraph of the same Report, showing that out of every 1000 girls of the age of 10 or under, 58 are already married, as against 22 boys. Taking Hindus alone, the number of married girls of 10 years of age or under is 70 per 1000 as against 28 married boys. Even allowing for those provinces where cohabitation is delayed, these figures mean in other provinces a cruel wrong to the children of the weaker sex, a doubly cruel wrong when to premature marriage may be added girl widowhood. The *Census Report* declares that in the lower strata of Hindu society there has been a rapid extension of child marriage and prohibition of the marriage of widows within the last two or three generations, although at the low age of 10, fewer girls are reported married than in 1881.[25] That is to say, the bad example of the higher castes is lowering the marriage age in the humble castes, while modern influences are diminishing the number of marriages of mere children,—we can see both forces in operation. Here again Indian Christians, Brāhmas, and Āryas are at one in setting a better example and advocating reform. The educative Act of 1891 for British India has also been noted above. Native States too are following up. In Rajputana, through the influence of the Agent of the Governor-General, Colonel Walter, an association was formed in 1888 which fixed the marriage age for two of the chief castes at eighteen for the bridegroom and fourteen for the bride. In the Native State of Baroda, in the extreme West of India, a new Marriage Act has just been passed by the enlightened ruler [1904]. In Baroda, except in special cases, the minimum marriage age of girls is henceforward to be twelve, and of the bridegrooms sixteen. Exceptional cases had to be provided for, because of the custom in certain communities within the state of Baroda to celebrate marriages only once every twelve years, female infants and girls of ten and twelve being then "happily despatched" together. With that custom and with the new Act together, it would necessarily happen that girls of eleven at the general marrying time would have to wait twelve years more, or until their twenty-third year. Since in some parts of India there is a saying about women "Old at twenty," that delay would not do. All educated young men may be said to hold the new ideas in these marriage matters. Students now regard it with regret and some sense of a grievance when their guardians have married them in their school or college years. The only alleviation to their minds is when the dowry which they bring into the family at their marriage helps to endow a sister who has reached the marriage age, or to educate a brother or pay off the family debts. Among educated people too, the idea that the other world is closed to bachelors and childless men has died, although a daughter unmarried after the age of puberty is still a stigma on the family. Do British readers realise that in an Indian novel of the middle and upper classes there can hardly be a bride older than twelve; there can be no love story of the long wooing and waiting of the lovers?

## Polygamy.

As regards polygamy, the Census shows 1011 married women for every 1000 married men, so that apparently not more than 11 married men in every 1000 are polygamists. But polygamy is still an Indian institution, in the sense that it is at the option of any man to have more than one wife; in the matter of marriage, the rights of man alone are regarded. All over India, however, among the educated classes, Mahomedans excepted, public opinion is now requiring a justification for a second marriage, as, for example, the barrenness, insanity, infirmity, or misconduct of the first spouse. The temptation of a second dowry is still, however, operative with men of certain high castes in which bridegrooms require to be paid for. The writer well remembers the pitiful comic tale of a struggling brahman student of Bengal, whose home had been made unhappy by the advent of two stepmothers in succession alongside of his own mother. The young man did not blame his father, for his father disapproved of polygamy, and was a polygamist only because he could not help himself. It had come about in an evil hour when he was desperate for a dowry for his eldest daughter, now come of marriageable age. He had listened to the village money-lender's advice that he might take a second wife himself and transfer to the daughter the dowry that the second wife would bring. Then in like manner the lapse of time had brought a second daughter to the marriage age, the necessity for another dowry, and a third mother into the student's home. The poor fellow himself was married too, and one could not resist the conjecture that *his* marriage was another sacrifice for the family, and that his marriage had saved his father from bringing home yet another stepmother. The redeeming feature of the story—the strength of Indian family ties—let us not be blind to.

Polygamy in India is certainly now hiding itself. A couple of generations ago it was practised wholesale by the kulin brahmans of Bengal. Several middle-aged kulins are known to have had more than 100 wives, and to have spent their lives in a round of visits to their numerous fathers-in-law. For each wife they had received a handsome bridegroom-price. So declares the last *Census Report*. Except among Indian Mahomedans, who have the sanction of the Koran and the example of the Prophet himself, there are now few upholders of polygamy in India. In a meeting of educated gentlemen in Calcutta a Mahomedan lately protested against some passing condemnatory reference to polygamy, on the ground that in a general meeting he expected that his religion would be free from attack. A learned Mahomedan judge, on the other hand, writes that among Indian Mahomedans "the feeling against polygamy is becoming a strong social if not a moral conviction." "Ninety-five out of every 100 are either by conviction or necessity monogamists." "It has become customary," he tells us, "to insert in the marriage deed a clause by which the intending husband formally renounces his supposed right to contract a second union."[26]

---

Seclusion of women.

---

With regard to the seclusion of women, at some points the custom seems to be slowly yielding to Western ideas, although it is still practically true that Indian ladies are never seen in society and in the streets of Indian cities.[27] A different evolution, however, is still more manifest at this present time. It almost seems as if at first modern life were to bend to the custom of the seclusion of women rather than bend the custom to itself. The Lady Dufferin Association for Medical Aid to Indian Women is bringing trained medical women *into* the zenanas and harems, and every year is also seeing a larger number of Indian Christian and Brāhma ladies set up as independent practitioners, able to treat patients *within* the women's quarters. In the year 1905 a lady lawyer, Miss Cornelia Sorabjee, a Parsee Christian lady, was appointed by the Government of Bengal to be a legal adviser to the Bengal Court of *Wards*, or landowning minors. Zenana or harem ladies, e.g. the widowed mothers of the minors, would thus be able to consult a trained lawyer at first hand *within* the zenana or harem. Missionaries are discussing the propriety of authorising certain Christian women to baptize women converts *within* the zenanas.[28] Long ago missions organised zenana schools, and now native associations have begun to follow in their steps. In all Indian Christian churches, women of course are present at public worship, but they always sit *apart* from the men, a segregation even more strictly followed by the Brāhma Samāj or Indian Theistic Association. For the sake of zenana women, the Indian Museum in Calcutta is closed one day each week to the male sex, and in some native theatres there is a ladies gallery in which ladies may see and not be seen behind a curtain of thin lawn. Movement even towards a compromise, it is good to observe.

---

Prohibition of the marriage of widows.

---

The prohibition of the marriage of widows has already been referred to as bound up with caste ideas of marriage and with social standing, and as the most deeply rooted part of the social inferiority of women. By some at least the injustice has been acknowledged since many years. At Calcutta, between 1840 and 1850, Babu Mati Lal Seal promised Rs10,000 to any Hindu, poor or rich, who would marry a widow of his own faith, but no one came forward.[29] The late Pandit Iswar Chander Vidyasagar of Calcutta has also already been mentioned as a champion of the widow's rights. But though legalised in 1856, the cases of re-marriage among the higher castes of Hindus in any year can still be counted on the fingers of one hand. The *Report of the Census of India*, 1901, takes a gloomy view regarding the province of Bengal, the most forward in many respects, but the most backward in respect of child-marriage and prohibition of the marriage of widows. The latter custom, we are told, "shows signs of extending itself far beyond its present limits, and finally of suppressing widow marriage throughout the entire Hindu community of Bengal."[30] The actual number of widows in all India in 1901 was 25,891,936, or about 2 out of every 11 of the female population, more than twice the proportion [1 in 13] in Great Britain. As in the matters of the repudiation of caste and the raising of the marriage age, the three new religious bodies, namely, the Indian Christians, the Brahmas, and the Āryas, stand side by side for the right of the widow.

# CHAPTER VI

## THE TERMS WE EMPLOY

"Precise ideas and precisely defined words are the wealth and the currency of the mind."

—Introduction to *The Pilgrim's Progress,* Macmillan's Edition.

> No *Indian* race or religion.

Experience teaches the necessity of explaining to Western readers certain terms which even long residence in India often fails to make clear to Anglo-Indians. Let it be remembered then that the terms *India, Indian,* have only a geographical reference: they do not signify any particular race or religion. India is the great triangular continent bounded on the south-west and south-east by the sea, and shut in on the north by the Himalayan Mountains. Self-contained though it be, and easily thought of as a geographical unit, we must not think of India as a racial, linguistic, or religious unit. We may much more correctly speak of *the* European race, language, or religion, than of *the* Indian.

> A Hindu religion.

The term *Hindu* refers to one of the Indian religions, the religion of the great majority no doubt. It is not now a national or geographical term. Practically every Hindu is an Indian, and almost necessarily must be so, but every Indian is not a Hindu. There are Indian Mahomedans, sixty-two million of them; Indian Buddhists, a few—the great majority of the Buddhists in the "Indian Empire" being in Burmah, not in India proper; there are Indian Christians, about three million in number; and there are Indian Parsees. A Hindu is the man who professes Hinduism.[31]

> Where is Hindustan?

*Hindustan,* or the land of the Hindus, is a term that never had any geographical definiteness. In the mouths of Indians it meant the central portion of the plain of North India; in English writers of half a century ago it was often used when all India was meant. In exact writing of the present time, the term is practically obsolete.

## Who speak Hindustani?

Unfortunately for clearness, the term *Hindustani* not only survives, but survives in a variety of significations. The word is an adjective, *pertaining to Hindustan*, and in English it has become the name either of the people of Hindustan or of their language. It is in the latter sense that the name is particularly confusing. The way out of the difficulty lies in first associating *Hindustani* clearly with the central region of Hindustan, the country to the north-east of Agra and Delhi. These were the old imperial capitals, be it remembered. Then from that centre, the Hindustani language spread—a central, imperial, Persianised language not necessarily superseding the other vernaculars—wherever the authority of the empire went. Thus throughout India, Hindustani became a *lingua franca*, the imperial language. In the Moghul Empire of Northern India it was exactly what "King's English" was in the Anglo-Norman kingdom in England in the thirteenth and fourteenth centuries. French was the language of the Anglo-Norman court of London, as Persian of the court of Delhi or Agra; the Frenchified King's English was the court form of the vernacular in England, as the Persianised Hindustani in North India. It was this *lingua franca* that Europeans in India set themselves to acquire.

## Urdu literature

Continuing the English parallel—the Hindustani of Delhi, the capital, Persianised as the English of London was Frenchified, became the recognised literary medium for North India. The special name *Urdu*, however, has now superseded the term *Hindustani*, when we think of the language as a literary medium. *Urdu* is the name for literary Hindustani; in the Calcutta University Calendar, for example, the name *Hindustani* never occurs.

## Hindi language and literature

About the beginning of the nineteenth century another dialect of Hindustani, called *Hindi*, also gained a literary standing. It contains much less of Persian than Urdu does, leaning rather to Sanscrit; it is written in the deva-nagari or Sanscrit character; is associated with Hindus and with the eastern half of Hindustan; whereas Urdu is written in the Persian character, and is associated with Mahomedans and the western half of Hindustan.[32]

## The Brahmans

Another series of terms are likewise a puzzle to the uninitiated. To Westerns, the *brahmans*[33] are best known as the priests of the Hindus; more correctly, however, the name *brahman* signifies not the performer of priestly duties, but the caste that possesses a monopoly of the performance. The brahman caste is the Hindu *Tribe of Levi*. Every accepted Hindu priest is a brahman, although it is far from being the case that every brahman is a priest. As a matter of fact, at the Census of 1901 it was found that the great majority of brahmans have turned aside from their traditional calling. In Bengal proper, only about 16 per cent. of the brahmans were following priestly pursuits; in the Madras Presidency, 11.4 per cent.; and in the Bombay Presidency, 22 per cent.

## Brahmanism.

*Brahmanism* is being employed by a number of recent writers in place of the older *Hinduism*. Sir Alfred Lyall uses *Brahmanism* in that sense; likewise Professor Menzies in his recent book, *Brahmanism and Buddhism*. Sir Alfred Lyall's employment of the term *Brahmanism* rather than *Hinduism*, is in keeping with his description of Hinduism, which he defines as the congeries of diverse local beliefs and practices that are held together by the employment of brahmans as priests. The description is a true one; the term Brahmanism represents what is common to the Hindu castes and sects; it is their greatest common measure, as it were. But yet the fact remains that *Hindus* speak of themselves as such, not as *Brahmanists*, and it is hopeless to try to supersede a current name. Sir M. Monier Williams employs the term *Brahmanism* in a more limited and more legitimate sense. Dividing the history of the Hindu religion into three periods, he calls them the stages of Vedism, Brahmanism, and Hinduism respectively. The first is the period of the Vedas, or earliest sacred books; the second, of the Brahman philosophy, fundamentally pantheistic; the third is the period of "a confused tangle of divine personalities and incarnations." Sir M. Monier Williams' standard work on the religion of the Hindus is "*Brahmanism and Hinduism.*" "Hinduism," he tells us, "is Brahmanism modified by the creeds and superstitions of Buddhists and non-Aryans of all kinds."

## Brahmā, Brahma.

We are not done with this confusing set of terms. *Brahmā* is the first person of the Hindu divine triad—the Creator—who along with the other two persons of the triad, has proceeded from a divine essence, *Brahma* or *Brahm*. Brahma is Godhead or Deity: Brahmā, is *a* Deity, a divine *person* who has emanated from the Godhead, Brahma. *Brāhmas* or theists, believers in Brahma, are a religious body that originated in Bengal in the nineteenth century. Repudiating caste, idolatry, and transmigration, they are necessarily cut off from Hinduism. The body is called the Brāhma Samāj, that is, the Theistic Association. Enough for the present; in their respective places these distinctions can be more fully gone into.

# CHAPTER VII

## NEW POLITICAL IDEAS

### I. A UNITING INDIA

"There are many nations of the Indians, and they do not speak the same language."

—HERODOTUS.[34]

---

The ideas of citizenship and public questions.

---

With modern education and the awakening of the Indian mind have come entirely new political ideas. That there are public questions has in fact been discovered; for in India the idea of citizenship, the consciousness of being a political unit, was itself a new idea. We may say that it was made possible in 1835, when an Act of Legislature was passed declaring the press free. In 1823 an English editor had been deported from Calcutta for free criticism of the authorities, but after 1835 it was legal not merely to think but to speak on public questions. Before we pass on, we note the strange inverted sequence of events which may attend on fostered liberty. The right to criticise was bestowed before any right to be represented in the Legislature or Executive was enjoyed. In this freedom to criticise the acts of Government, the India of to-day is far ahead of countries like Germany and Russia.

---

Government exists for the good of the governed.

---

The new idea of citizenship, thus made possible by a free press, is largely the outcome of three great influences. Christian philanthropic ideas, disseminated both by precept and example, could not but be producing some sense of brotherhood, and what Burke calls a "civil society." Then again, the free and often democratic spirit of English literature was being imbibed by thousands; and in the third place, through the newspapers, English and vernacular, the people were being brought into actual contact with the political life of Great Britain. Due particularly to the first of these influences, the noblest of the new Indian political ideas is that tacitly assumed in many of the native criticisms of the British Government in India—high tribute as well as criticism—that Government exists for the good of the governed, and indeed responsible for the welfare of the masses. The British Government is indeed an amazing network covering the whole continent, ministering life, like the network of the blood-vessels in our frame. At least, its apologists declare it *to be doing so*, and its native critics declare that it *ought to*. The native press, for example, is prompt to direct the attention of the Government to famine and to summon the Government to its duty. In India a noble idea of the Commonwealth and its proper government has thus come into being. Likewise, it ought to be added, except in times of political excitement, and in the case of professional politicians, it is generally acknowledged that the conception of the British Government in India is noble, and that many officers of Government are truly the servants of the people. It is not suggested that the policy or the methods should be radically altered. The politician's theme is that the Government is more expensive and less sympathetic than it might be, because of the employment of alien Europeans where natives might be employed.

The new national consciousness.

English rule, a chief cause.

The very name *Indian* is English.

Other new political ideas follow the lines of social change. We have seen how in the modern school, the idea of caste gives way before the idea of rank in the school, to be followed in College by the idea of intellectual distinction, and still later in life by the idea of success in some modern career. In the political sphere, modern life is also busy dissolving the older and narrower conceptions of life. Atop of the sectarian consciousness of being a Hindu or the provincial consciousness of belonging to Bengal or Bombay, is coming the consciousness of being an Indian. This consciousness of a national unity is one of the outstanding features of the time in India, all the more striking because hitherto India has been so unwieldily large, and her people incoherent, like dry sand. "The Indian never knew the feeling of nationality," says Max Müller. "The very name of India is a synonym for caste, as opposed to nationality," says Sister Nivedita, the pro-Hindu lady already referred to, who likewise notes the emergence of the national idea.[35] "Public spirit or patriotism, as we understand it, never existed among the Hindus," writes Mr. Bose, himself an Indian, author of a recent work on *Hindu Civilisation under British Rule.*[36] And Raja Rammohan Roy, the famous Bengali reformer of the beginning of the nineteenth century, we have already heard denouncing the caste system as "destructive of national union." From what then, during the nineteenth century, has the national consciousness come forth? Many causes may be cited. The actual unification effected by the postal, the telegraph, and the railway organisation, has done much. The omnipresence of the foreign government, all-controlling, has also done much. The current coins and the postage stamps with King Edward's head upon them—the same all over India, a few native states excepted—bring home the union of India to the most ignorant. The constant criticism of the Government in the native press, the meetings of the All-India political association called the Congress, and the fact that modern interests, stimulated by daily telegrams from all over the world, are international, not provincial or sectarian—all these things combine to give to the modern educated Indian a new Indian national consciousness in place of the old provincial and sectarian one. In short, the British rule has united India, and the awakened mind of India is rejoicing in the consciousness of the larger existence, and is identifying the ancient glories of certain centres in North India with this new India created by Britain. Never before was there a united India in the modern political sense; never, indeed, could there be until modern inventions brought distant places near each other. Two great Indian empires there certainly were in the third century B.C. and the fourth and fifth centuries A.D., and the paternal benevolence of Asoka, the great Buddhist emperor of the third century B.C., deserves record and all honour. Let Indians know definitely who deserves to be called an ancient Indian emperor, when they wish to lament a lost past; and descending to historical fact and detail, let them compare that period with the present. The later empire referred to was an empire only in the old sense of a collection of vassal states. Turning back to the hoary past, in which many Indians, even of education, imagine there was a golden Indian empire, we can trace underneath the ancient epic, the Ramayan, a conquering progress southward to Ceylon itself of a great Aryan hero, Ram. But of any Indian empire founded by him, we know nothing. "One who has carefully studied the Ramayan will be impressed with the idea that the Aryan conquest had spread over parts of Northern India only, at the time of the great events which form its subjects."[37] Coming down to the period of the greatest extent of the Moghul empire in India in the end of the seventeenth century, we find the Emperor Aurangzeb with as extensive a military empire as that of Asoka, but with the Mahrattas rising behind him even while he was extending his empire southwards. That decadent military despotism cannot be thought of as a union of India. In truth, the old Aryan conquest of India was not a political conquest, and never has been; it was a conquest, very complete in the greater part of India, of new social usages and certain new religious ideas. The first complete political conquest of India by Aryans was the British conquest, and the ideas which have come in or been awakened thereby, we are now engaged in tracing. As regards the new idea of nationality, we have noted that the new national name *Indian* now heard upon political platforms, is not a native term, but an importation from Britain along with the English language. How, indeed, could the educated Indian employ any other term with the desired comprehensiveness? If he speak of *Hindus*, he excludes Mahomedans and followers of other religions; if he use a Sanscrit term for *Indians*, he still fails to touch the hearts of Mahomedans and others who identify Sanscrit with Hindus. There is no course left but to use the English language, even while criticising the British rulers. The English language has been a prime factor in evoking the new national consciousness, and in the English language the Indian must speak to his new found fellow Indians.[38] Even a considerable portion of the literature of the attempted Revival of Hinduism is in English, strange as the conjunction sounds.

How the thought of Indian unity over against the sovereignty of Britain may reach down even to the humblest, the writer once observed in a humble street in Calcutta. A working man was receiving his farthing's worth of entertainment from a peep-show. His eyes were glued to the peepholes, to secure his money's worth, for the farthing was no small sum to him; and the showman was standing by describing the successive scenes in a loud voice, with intent both to serve his customer and to stimulate the bystanders' curiosity. Three of the scenes were: "This is the house of the great Queen near London city," "This is one of the great Queen's lords writing an order to the Viceroy of Calcutta," "This is the great committee that sits in London city." He actually used the English word *committee*, the picture probably showing the House of Commons or the House of Lords. Thus the political constitution of India and its unity under Britain are inculcated among the humblest. In the minds of the educated, one need not then be surprised at the growth of a sense of Indian unity over against British supremacy.

The Indian National Congress.

English, the *lingua franca* of the Congress.

The Indian National Congress, or All-India political association, is the embodiment of this new national consciousness of educated Indians, the only embodiment possible while India is so divided in social and religious matters. Were there only ten or twelve million Mahomedans in India instead of sixty, the new national consciousness would undoubtedly have been a Hindu or religious, instead of a political, consciousness. But in matters religious, Hindu looks across a gulf at Mahomedan, and Mahomedan at Hindu, neither expecting the other to cross over. Christianity, third in numbers in India proper, proclaims the Christian Gospel to both Hindus and Mahomedans, but is regarded by both as an alien.[39] Nor is any All-India *social* movement possible while social differences are so sacred as they are. But politically, all India *is* already *one*; her educated men have drunk at *one* well of political ideas; citizenship and its rights are attractive and destroy no cherished customs; and in the English language there is a new *lingua franca* in unison with the new ideas. The Indian National Congress is the natural outcome. There, representatives of races which a hundred years ago made war on one another, of castes that never either eat together or intermarry, now fraternise in one peaceful assembly, inspired by the novel idea that they are citizens. The Congress meets annually in December in one or other of the cities of India. The first meeting at Bombay in 1885 has been described as follows[40]: "There were men from Madras, the blackness of whose complexions seemed to be made blacker by spotless white turbans which some of them wore. A few others hailing from the same Presidency were in simplest native fashion, bareheaded and barefooted and otherwise lightly clad, their bodies from the waist upwards being only partially protected by muslin shawls. They had preferred to retain their national dress and manners; and in this respect they presented a marked contrast to the delegates from Bengal. Some of these appeared in entirely European costume, while others could easily be recognised as Bengalis by the peculiar cap with a flap behind which they had donned. None of them wore the gold rings or diamond pendants which adorned the ears of some of the Madrassees; nor had they their foreheads painted like their more orthodox and more conservative brethren from the Southern presidency. There were Hindustanis from Delhi, Agra, and Lucknow, some of whom wore muslin skull-caps and dresses chiefly made of the same fine cloth. There were delegates from the North-West—bearded, bulky, and large-limbed men—in their coats and flowing robes of different hues, and in turbans like those worn by Sikh soldiers. There were stalwart Sindhees from Karachee wearing their own tall hat surmounted by a broad brim at top instead of bottom. In the strange assemblage were to be observed the familiar figures of Banyas from Gujarat, of Mahrattas in their cart-wheel turbans, and of Parsees in their not very elegant head-dress, likened to a slanting roof.

Assembled in the same hall, they presented a variety of costumes and complexions scarcely to be witnessed except at a fancy ball." Now and again, we may add, a speaker expresses himself in a vernacular, and with the inborn Indian courtesy and patience the assembly will listen; but the language of the motley gathering is English; the address of the president and his rulings are in English; the protests, claims, and resolutions of the Congress are in English. For in the sphere of politics, the new national feeling *confessedly* looks to Britain for ideals. Apologies for India's social customs and for her religious ideas and ideals are not wanting in India at the present time, for in matters social and religious, as we shall see, the political reformers are often ardently conservative, or pro-Indian at least. But in the sphere of politics it is the complete democratic constitution of Britain that looms before India's leaders. Britons can view with sympathy the rise of the national feeling as the natural and inevitable fruit of contact with Britain and of education in the language of freedom, and even although the new problems of Indian statesmanship may call forth all the powers of British statesmen. Like a young man conscious of noble lineage and of great intellectual power, New India, brought up under Britain's care, is loudly asserting that she can now take over the management of the continent which Britain has unified and made what it is.

Where the "National Congress" and the Congress ideas have sprung from is manifest when she first presents herself upon the Indian stage. As her first president she has a distinguished barrister of Calcutta, Mr. W.C. Bonnerjee, of brahman caste by birth, but out of caste altogether because of frequent visits to Britain. Patriot though he is—nay, rather, as a true patriot, he has broken and cast away the shackles of caste. His English education is manifest when he opens his lips, for in India there is no more complete master of the English language, and very few greater masters will be found even in Britain. Further, as her first General Secretary and general moving spirit, the first Congress has a Scotchman, Mr. A.O. Hume, commonly known as the "Father of the Congress." His leading of the Congress we can understand when we know that he is the son of the celebrated reformer and member of Parliament, the late Dr. Joseph Hume.

Representative Government.

Several of the claims of the Congress have been conceded in whole or in part. Since the first meeting in 1885, elected members have been added to the Legislative Councils in the three chief provinces, Bengal, Madras, and Bombay, and new Legislative Councils set up in the United Provinces and the Punjab. To the Council for all India, the Viceroy's Council, also have been added five virtually elected members, out of a council now numbering about twenty-two members in all. Four of the new members represent the chief provinces, and the fifth the Chamber of Commerce, Calcutta. Other five the Viceroy nominates to represent other provinces or other interests. Looking at the representation of Indians, it is noteworthy that in 1880 only two Indians had seats in the Viceroy's Council, whereas in 1905 there were no fewer than six. The Provincial Legislative Council of Bombay will suffice as illustration of the stage which Representative Government has now reached. Eight of the twenty-two members are virtually elected. That is to say, certain bodies nominate representatives, and only in most exceptional circumstances would the Governor refuse to accept the nominees. And who make the nominations? Who are the electors enjoying the new political citizenship of India? We shall not expect that the electors are "the people" in the British or American sense: no Congress yet asks for political rights for them. The idea regarding citizenship still is that it is a royal concession, as it were to royal burghs, not that it is one of the rights of men. The University elects a member to the Governor's Council, for it has intelligence and can make its voice heard; the Corporation of Bombay elects a representative, for in the capital are concentrated the enlightenment and the wealth of the province; the importance of the British merchants must be recognised, and so the Chambers of Commerce of Bombay and Karachi send each a representative. Other groups of municipalities elect one; the boards of certain country districts elect one; and finally two groups of landlords elect one representative each. It comes to this, that the men of learning, the burgesses of the chief towns, the British traders, and the landowners and country gentlemen, have now a measure of citizenship in the modern sense of the word.

The same feeling of citizenship has been given recognition to in 759 towns, whose municipalities are now partly elected, the right of election having been greatly extended by the Local Self-Government Acts of 1882-84. In these Municipalities even more than in the higher Councils the new educated Indian comes to the front. According to the roll of voters, it is property that enjoys the municipal franchise; emphatically so, for a wealthy citizen of Calcutta might conceivably cast three hundred votes for his Municipality throughout the twenty-five wards of the city; but they are English-speaking Indians in all cases who are returned as members. Politically, this is the day of the English-educated Indians. Such is the stage of the recognition of this new idea of citizenship in India. The idea represents a great advance during the British period, although, broadly speaking, it has not yet reached the stage of British opinion prior to 1832. Nevertheless one feels justified in saying that in present circumstances the desire of the educated class for a measure of citizenship has been reasonably met. Of course at the examination for the Indian Civil Service, held annually in London, the Indian competes on a complete equality with all the youth of the Empire.

# CHAPTER VIII

## NEW POLITICAL IDEAS

### II. FALSE PATRIOTISM

"Now do I know that love is blind."

ALFRED AUSTIN.

---
Cleavage of opinion—European *v.* Native.

---

An unpleasant aspect of the new idea is much in evidence at the present time. On almost every public question, the cleavage of the public opinion is Europeans *versus* Natives. Far be it from me to assert that the natives only are carried away by the community feeling. A case in point is the violence of the European agitation over the "Ilbert Bill" of 1883, to permit trial of Europeans by native judges in rural criminal courts. Our question merely is: How has the new regime affected native ideas? Given then, say, a charge of assault upon a native by a European or Eurasian, or the reverse—a case by no means unknown—the native press and the class they represent are ranged at once, as a matter of course, upon the native's side. Given a great public matter, like Lord Curzon's Bill of 1903 for the necessary reform of the Indian Universities, immediately educated Indians and the native press perceive in it a veiled attempt to limit the higher education in order to diminish the political weight of the educated class. The 1904 expedition into Thibet was unanimously approved by the Anglo-Indian, and as unanimously disapproved by the native press. Educated India no doubt joined with the rest of the Empire in wishing success to Japan in the 1904-5 war with Russia, but the war presented itself primarily to the Indian mind as a great struggle between Asia and Europe. Other lines of cleavage may temporarily show themselves,—among natives the division into Hindus and Mahomedans, or into officials and non-officials; but on the first occasion when a European and a Native are opposed, or when the Government takes any step, the minor fissures close, and the new consciousness of nationality unites the Indians. European lines of cleavage like the division between capital and labour or between commerce and land have not yet risen above the Indian horizon.

The Indian Christian community occupies the peculiar position of sharing in the new-born national consciousness as strongly as any, and yet of being identified with the British side in the eyes of the Hindu and Mahomedan communities.

> Anti-British bias.

> India ruled by Indians.

Thus, almost inevitably, an anti-British bias has been generated, one of the noteworthy and regrettable changes in the Indian mind within the last half-century. Probably many would declare that the unifying national consciousness of which I have spoken is nothing more than a racial anti-British bias. At all events, hear an independent Indian witness regarding the bias.[41] "There is a strong and strange ferment working in certain ranks of Indian society.... Instead of looking upon the English rulers as their real benefactors, they are beginning to view their actions suspiciously, seizing every opportunity of criticising and censuring their rulers.... The race feeling between rulers and ruled, instead of diminishing, has increased with the increase, and spread with the spread, of literary education. That all this is more or less true at present cannot be denied by an impartial political observer." An up-to-date illustration of the bias appears in the address of the Chairman of the National Congress of 1906. "The educated classes," he says, "... now see clearly that the [British] bureaucracy is growing frankly selfish and openly opposed to their political aspirations." While regretting that feeling and the prejudice that often mingles with it, let those interested in India at least understand the feeling. It is the natural outcome of the new national consciousness. Even educated natives are in general too ignorant of India, past and present, to appreciate the debt of India to Britain, and how great a share of the administration of India they themselves—the educated Indians—actually enjoy. For every subordinate executive position in the vast imperial organisation is held by a native of India, and "almost the entire original jurisdiction of Civil Justice has passed out of the hands of Europeans into those of Indians."[42] But the anti-British bias, let us on our part understand. The attitude of educated Indians to the British Government of India, and to Anglo-Indians as a body, is that of a political opposition, ignorant of many pertinent facts, divided from the party in power by racial and religious differences, and with no visible prospect of succeeding to office. The National Congress is the permanent Opposition in India. A permanent Opposition cannot but be biassed, and its press will seize at everything that will justify the feeling of hostility.

An outstanding illustration of the anti-British spirit is the frequently expressed opinion that the Indian famines are a result of British rule, or at all events have been aggravated thereby. The reasoning is that India is being financially drained to the amount of between thirty and forty millions sterling a year, and that the people of India have thus no staying fund to keep them going when famine comes. Having said this, we ought perhaps to quote the opinion (1903), on the other side, of Mr. A.P. Sinnett, ex-editor of one of the leading Indian newspapers, and, as a theosophist, very unlikely to be prejudiced in favour of Britain. He insists "that loss of life in famine time is infinitesimal compared with what it used to be." "As for impoverishment," he goes on to say, "we have poured European capital into the country by scores of millions for public works and the establishment of factories, and we have enriched India instead of impoverishing it to an extent that makes the Home Charges—of which such agitators as Digby always exaggerate the importance—a mere trifle in the balance." Lord Curzon's statement of three or four years back was that there were eight hundred and twenty-five crores of rupees (five hundred and fifty millions sterling) of buried capital in India; and he might have added the easily ascertainable fact that the sum is yearly being added to. The anti-British idea was put forward in 1885 by the late Mr. William Digby, an ardent supporter of the Congress; the Congress adopted it in one of its resolutions in 1896, and the idea has lamentably caught on. In 1897 a Conference of Indians resident in London did not mince their language. In their opinion, "of all the evils and terrible misery that India has been suffering for a century and a half, and of which the latest developments are the most deplorable famine and plague arising from ever-increasing poverty,... the main cause is the unrighteous and un-British system of Government, which produces an unceasing and ever increasing bleeding of the country," etc. etc.[43] Such language, such ideas, do not call for refutation, here at least; they are symptoms only of a state of mind now prevailing, out of which educated India must surely grow.

Nor need it be forgotten that the rise of the anti-British feeling was foreseen and political danger apprehended when the question of English education for natives of India was under discussion. A former Governor-General, Lord Ellenborough, declared to a committee of the House of Commons in 1852, that England must not expect to retain her hold on India if English ideas were imparted to the people. "No *intelligent* people would submit to our Government," were his words—a sentiment repudiated with indignation by the learned Bengali, the late Rev. Dr. K.M. Banerjea. In the same spirit, apparently, Sir Alfred Lyall still contemplates with some fear the rapid reformation of religious beliefs under modern influences. He sees that the old deities and ideas are being dethroned, and that the responsibility for famines, formerly imputed to the gods, is being cast upon the British Government. "The British Government," he says, "having thrown aside these lightning conductors [the old theocratic system], is much more exposed than a native ruler would be to shocks from famines or other wide-spread misfortunes." "Where no other authority is recognised, the visible ruler becomes responsible for everything."[44] Fortunately, "policy" of that sort has not prevailed with Indian statesmen in the past, and Britain can still retain self-respect as enlightener and ruler of India.

Championing of things Indian.

The championing of all things Indian is another recent phase of the same national consciousness. As the work of Britain is depreciated, the heroes, the beliefs, and the practices of India are exalted and defended as such. Idolatry and caste have their apologists. At almost every public meeting, according to the late Mr. Monomohun Ghose of Calcutta, he heard the remark made "that the ancient civilisation of India was far superior to that which Europe ever had."[45] In the political lament over a golden past, there is glorification by Hindus of the Mahomedan emperor Akbar, praise of the Native States and their rule as opposed to the condition of British India, and there are apologies for leaders in the Mutiny of 1857. Much of that is natural and proper patriotism, no doubt, and no one would deny the ancient glories of India or the many admirable characteristics of the people of India to-day. It is the self-deceiving patriotism, the blind ancestor-worship, of which we are speaking as a phase of modern opinion. As an instance when Indians certainly did themselves injustice by this spirit, we may single out the celebrated trial in 1897 of the Hon. Mr. Tilak, member of the Legislative Council of the Governor of Bombay. The Mahrattas of Western India look back to Sivaji as the founder of their political power, which lasted down to 1817, and have lately instituted an annual celebration of Sivaji as the hero of the Mahratta race. One great blot rests on Sivaji's career. In one campaign he invited the Mahomedan general opposing him to a personal conference, and stabbed him while in the act of embracing him. It was at one of these Sivaji celebrations in 1897 that Mr. Tilak abandoned himself to the pro-Indian and anti-British feeling, glorifying Sivaji's use of the knife upon foreigners. "Great men are above common principles of law," ... he said. "In killing Afzal Khan did Sivaji sin?" ... "In the Bhagabat Gita," he replied to himself, "Krishna has counselled the assassination of even one's preceptors and blood relations.... If thieves enter one's house, and one's wrists have no strength to drive them out, one may without compunction shut them in and burn them. God Almighty did not give a charter ... to the foreigners to rule India, Sivaji strove to drive them out of his fatherland, and there is no sin of covetousness in that." Practical application of Mr. Tilak's language was soon forthcoming in the assassination of two British officers in the same city of Poona. Mr. Tilak, victim of his own eloquence and of the spirit of the day, was necessarily prosecuted for his inflammatory speech, and was sent to prison for eighteen months. But it is not too much to say that the *unanimous* feeling of educated India went with Mr. Tilak and regarded him as a martyr.

---

Boycott of British goods.

---

From the pro-Indian feeling to the anti-British Boycott feeling is only one step along the road that new-educated India is treading. The boycott of British goods in 1905 has been the next step. The provocation alleged by the politicians who organised the boycott was the division of the province of Bengal. Whether that was cause sufficient to justify the boycott or a mere pretext for another anti-British step is now of secondary importance. The plea of encouragement of native industries we may set aside as an afterthought. The boycott has been declared, and what concerns us is to see the national feeling now take the form of a declaration of commercial war upon Great Britain—none the less disconcerting because some of those concerned clearly have an eye, however foolishly, upon Boston in 1773 and the war thereafter. It gives pause to India's well-wishers. "India for the Indians," will that come next? There no friend of India dare wish her success, to be a possible prey to Russia or Germany, or even to Japan. But reasoning to the logical issue, we get light upon our premisses. *India for what Indians?*, we ask ourselves. For Hindus or Mahomedans; for the million, English-speaking, or the many-millioned masses? For many a day yet to come it will be Britain's duty to hold the balance, to instruct in self-government and to learn from her blunders.

That the national feeling of Indians may become a main strand in a strong Imperial feeling, as is the national feeling of Scotland, must be the wish of all friends of India. But how is the Indian feeling to be transformed?

---

Remedies.

---

---

Instruction in History and Political Economy.

---

The new Social Ideas of India have asserted themselves in spite of opposing ideas, deep-rooted; on the other hand, the new Political Ideas are in accordance with the natural ambition of educated Indians, and have had no difficulty in expanding and spreading. In comparison with the new social ideas, in consequence, the new political ideas are a somewhat rank and artificial growth, forced by editors and politicians, and warped by ignorance and prejudice. The widely current idea that, owing to British rule, the poverty of the Indian people is now greater, and that the famines are more frequent and severe than in former dynasties, is the outstanding instance of the rank growth. Neither the allegation of greater poverty nor the causes of the acknowledged low standard of living have been studied except in the fashion of party politicians. Another of the ideas, as widely current, is that every ton of rice or wheat exported is an injury to the poor. A third is that the payments made in Britain by the Government of India are virtually tribute, meanly exacted, instead of honest payment for cash received and for services rendered. Again, what can be the remedy? In the early part of the nineteenth century, the Foreign Mission Committee of the Church of Scotland objected to Dr. Duff, their missionary, teaching Political Economy in the Church's Mission College, the General Assembly's Institution, Calcutta. They feared lest the East India Company would deem it an interference in politics.[46] In 1897, after the Tilak case already referred to, the writer on Indian affairs in *The Times* complained of the teaching of historical half-truths and untruths in Indian schools and colleges, instancing the partisan writings of Burke and Macaulay, and many Indian text-books full of glaring historical perversions. The remedy for such erroneous ideas is certainly not to withhold the present dole of knowledge, but to teach the whole truth. The recent History of India and Political Economy with reference to India should be compulsory subjects for every student in an Indian University. It ought to be the policy of Government to select the ablest men for professors and teachers of such subjects. If, along with that remedy, more Anglo-Indians would take a high view of their mission to India, and of their residence in that country, much of that regrettable bias and bitterness on the part of Indians would surely pass away. If instead of adopting the attitude of exiles, thinking only of the termination of the exile and how to while away the interval, Anglo-Indians would take some interest in something Indian outside their business, much would be gained! The best Anglo-Indians are eager to promote intercourse between Europeans and Indians, but many Anglo-Indians, whatever the cause, seem incapable of friendly intercourse. On the matters that should interest both them and their fellow-citizens in India, they have in them nothing save unreasoned feelings. These form the numerous class, of whom Sir Henry

Cotton spoke in an address in London in February 1904, to whom it is an offence to travel in the same railway-carriage with Indians. These are the corrupters of good feeling between Britons and Indians, as sympathetic men are the salt that preserves what good feeling may still exist. In every Indian sphere the men of the latter class are well known to the native community, and are always spoken of with cordiality. The writer remembers trying to have a talk with a British soldier about the generals of the army, and how the man seemed unable to do more than say, with enthusiasm, of Lord Roberts and General Wauchope and others, "Yon was a man!" and as depreciatorily of others again, "Yon was no man at all." Such sympathetic "men," instinctively discerned, India has much need of, if this anti-British feeling, so far as it is not inevitable, is to be checked. In such "men" the new Indian feelings of manhood and citizenship and nationality will find recognition and response, in spite of displeasing accompaniments, for such feelings we must look for under British rule and from English and Christian education. From such "men," also, the new Indians will accept frank condemnation of social irrationalities or political exaggerations, as *e.g.* the notion that those have right to claim full share in the British Empire's management who would outcaste a fellow-Indian for visiting Britain, even had he gone to state their case before the House of Commons. To speak of laymen only, there are no Anglo-Indians more trusted than those who make no secret of their desire for the advancement of India's welfare through a religious reformation, who hold that this purely pro-Indian national feeling is as yet imperfect because divorced from the idea of the unity of mankind and the concomitant idea of the progress of the whole race.

# CHAPTER IX

## NEW RELIGIOUS IDEAS—ARE THERE ANY?

"From low to high doth dissolution climb.

---

Truth fails not; but her outward forms that bear
The longest date do melt like frosty rime,
That in the morning whitened hill and plain
And is no more; drop like the tower sublime
Of yesterday, which royally did wear
His crown of weeds, but could not even sustain
Some casual shout that broke the silent air,
Or the unimaginable touch of Time."

WORDSWORTH.

---

A Renaissance without a reformation.

---

It would be interesting to speculate what the Renaissance of the sixteenth century would have done for Europe had it been unaccompanied by a Reformation of religion. Without the Reformation, we may aver there would have been for the British nation no Bible of 1611, no Pilgrim Fathers to America, and no Revolution of 1688, along with all that these things imply of progress many-fold. What might have been, however, although interesting as a speculation, is too uncertain to be discussed further with profit. I only desire to give a general idea of the religious situation in India at the close of the nineteenth century. There has been a Renaissance without a Reformation.

Into the new intellectual world the Hindu mind has willingly entered, but progress in religious ideas has been slow and reluctant. The new *political* idea of the unity of India and the consciousness of citizenship were pleasing discoveries that met with no opposition; but that same new Indian national consciousness resented any departure from the old *social* and *religious* ideas.

In speaking of the development of religious ideas in India, I use the term *religious* in the modern sense. Under religion, in India is comprehended much that in Europe would be reckoned within the *social* sphere. In India all questions of inter-marriage and of eating together, many questions regarding occupations and the relations of earning members of a family to idle members, are religious not social questions.

The case was similar among the Jews, we may remember. As recorded in the fifteenth chapter of the Acts of the Apostles, two of the three injunctions of the Jerusalem Church to the Gentile Church at Antioch deal with these same socio-religious matters. Blood and animals killed by strangling were to be prohibited as food, and certain marriages also were forbidden.

Perhaps among Europeans the question of burial *v.* cremation may be instanced as a matter of social custom that has been made a religious question. But in no country more than in India have customs, *mores*, come also to mean morals. A halo of religious sanctity encircles the things that have been and are. Taking "religion," however, in the modern sense, we ask: Although there has not been any great Reformation of religion, have religious ideas undergone no noteworthy development? It is well to put the question definitely with regard to religion, although in the opening chapter abundant testimony to a general change in ideas has already been cited. There *is* no lack of specific evidence as to religious changes, and the adoption of certain Christian ideas.

Sir Alfred Lyall's observations let us first of all recall, for he possesses all the experience of an Indian Civil Servant and Governor of a Province—the United Provinces. He speaks both for officials and for Europeans conversant with India.[47] Speaking in the person of an orthodox brahman surveying the moral and material changes that English rule is producing in India, he says: "We are parting rapidly under ... this Public Instruction with our religious beliefs." The old brahman warns the British Government that the old deities are being dethroned, and that the responsibility for famines, formerly imputed to the gods, is being cast upon the British Government. Another official witness speaks still more plainly. *The Bengal Government Report* upon the publications of the year 1899 asserts: "All this revolution in the religious belief of the educated Hindu has been brought about as much by the dissemination of Christian thought by missionaries as by the study of Hindu scriptures; for Christian influence is detectable in many of the Hindu publications of the year." The writer of the *Report* is a Hindu gentleman. The *Report of the Census of India*, 1901, declares that "the influence of

Christian teaching is ... far reaching, and that there are many whose acts and opinions have been greatly modified thereby." After these statements from secular and official writers, we may refrain from quoting from Mission authorities more than the statement of the Decennial Conference of representative missionaries from all India in 1902. The statement refers to South India. "Christianity," we are told, "is in the air. The higher classes are assimilating its ideas."[48] Thus from East and North and South, from officials and non-officials, from Europeans and natives, comes concurrent testimony. There is no declared Reformation, but Christian and Western religious ideas are leavening India.

---

Variety of religious ideas in India.

---

To the student of Comparative Religion, or of Christianity, or of the general progress of nations, that testimony from India is particularly interesting. To the student of Comparative Religion, India presents a particularly attractive field. Not hidden away in sacred classics or in the records of travellers, but as elements of existing religions, professed by men around, are illustrations of most of the types of religious thought and practice. There are the pantheism of certain Hindu ascetics, the polytheism of the masses, the animism of aboriginal races, and the varieties of theism of Christians, Mahomedans, and the new Hindus respectively. There are the curious phenomena of goddesses as well as gods, and of distinctive features in the character and worship of the female deities. There is the whole scale of worship up from bloody sacrifices and self-tortures and from worship where the priest is everything, to worship like that of Mahomedans and of Protestant Christians, where a mediatory priesthood is virtually repudiated. There is the stage, still farther beyond, at which the worshipper is supposed to be able to say of himself "I am God." Of the first and last stages, India may be called the special fields, for probably nowhere else in the world are so many animals killed in sacrifice as at the temple of Kalighat in Calcutta; and the last stage, as an observable religious phenomenon, is peculiar to India. In India there is presented to us salvation in the attainment of an eternal existence along with God, as among Christians and Mahomedans and many of the less educated Hindus; and there is salvation in deliverance from further lives, as among those Hindus who hold the doctrine of transmigration. In India all these varieties of religious thought and practice are actual, perceptible phenomena, ready for first-hand observation by the student of Comparative Religion. But still more interesting to him is that they are there in mutual contact, and telling upon each other. For in the sphere of human beliefs, the student is much more than an outside observer and classifier. He has his own conception of truth, and is interested in observing how far in each case there is a convergence towards truth or a divergence from it. In the sphere of human beliefs he holds further, that, given opportunity, the nearer to truth the greater certainty of survival. Given opportunity, as already postulated, the law of beliefs is the survival of the truest. Truth will prevail.

---
Dynamical elements of Christianity.
---

---
Dynamical doctrines in other spheres
---

To the student of Christianity, again, that same concurrent testimony is profoundly interesting. Certain Christian ideas are being assimilated in India. Certain cardinal aspects of Christianity are proving themselves possessed of inherent force and attractiveness. They are showing that they possess force not from authority, or tradition, or as part of a system of doctrine, or as racially fitting, but when presented in new and often very unfavourable surroundings. Borrowing an expression from physical science, certain elements of Christianity are proving *themselves dynamical*. For in non-Christian India, ecclesiastical authority or tradition and the system of Christian doctrine as such, possess no force. By illustrations from other spheres, let us make clear what is meant by such dynamical elements of Christianity. The doctrine of the Origin of Species by means of Natural Selection was put before the world by Darwin in 1859, and within the half century has been accepted almost as an axiom by the whole civilised world. Undoubtedly that doctrine has proved itself dynamical. On the other hand, a few years earlier than the publication of *The Origin of Species*, another body of new doctrine was propounded to Britain and the world, and strongly urged by its upholders, namely, the doctrine of Free Trade—the advantage to the community of buying in the cheapest market. True or false, that body of doctrine has not proved dynamical among the nations, for the great majority of peoples still repudiate the doctrines of Free Trade. Similarly certain elements of Christianity are commending themselves to new India, and certain others are failing to do so at this time.

---
Illustrations from the history of Christianity.
---

From century to century these dynamical elements of Christianity may vary; and it is profoundly interesting to the student of the history of religious beliefs to observe the variation. In the early apostolic times, when the apostles and disciples were "scattered abroad," we see plainly in the Acts of the Apostles that the dynamical element of Christianity is the Resurrection of Our Lord. It is that which tells, and His coming reign—

with Jewish audiences in particular. It was, *e.g.*, the manifestation of Christ to St. Paul on his way to Damascus that completed the conversion of his life. And so, repeatedly throughout the record of the Acts of the Apostles, they are described as witness—bearers of the resurrection to the outside world. [Greek: Megalê dynamei], "*with great power* gave the apostles their witness of the resurrection of the Lord Jesus; and great grace was upon them all."[49] And yet—dynamical elements vary—in the different atmosphere of Athens (we are twice told in so many words) this same resurrection of Christ dug a gulf between St. Paul and the Athenians.[50] Passing to a very different period, the latter half of the eighteenth century, the period of the rise of Methodism and the revival of religion in England, the period of new interest in the inmates of prisons, of agitation for the abolition of slavery, of the foundation of all the great missionary societies, the period of the French Revolution and the demand at home for extension of the franchise, all outcome of the same inspiration,—what was the strong epidemic thought? Reading the religious history of the time, we feel that the power that passed from soul to soul was a tremulously intense realisation of the family of God and the love of God for men, represented in Christ's voluntary death upon the cross, love for the neglected and the enslaved in their sins and their sorrows. And again in our own day, when we are tempted to say that the consciousness of God and the eternal, the primary religious instincts, are fading, what by common consent is really dynamical among educated men? Assuredly not the shibboleths of High or Low Church. It is the person of Jesus Christ that is dynamical; what He was on earth, what He has been ever since in the hearts of individuals and in the Church. In a real sense we are starting again from and with Himself. Anticipating, let us say that these two elements most recently dynamical in Britain have had force likewise in India.

---

India a new touch-stone of Christianity.

---

India in the nineteenth century has been indeed a new touchstone to the Christian religion; and, in brief, to make plain how far Christianity has proved its force and its fitness to survive will occupy the remaining chapters of this book. What has been the nature and extent of the impact of Christian and modern thought upon India, and particularly upon Hinduism? Of course I am thinking particularly of the educated native Hindu community that has sprung up during the century just closed. The dynamic of Christianity, which it is our task to test, implies a measure of conscious and intelligent approval. Japan is another such testing ground. Indeed the only large fields where Christianity is presented to bodies of non-Christian men able to yield approval or refuse it on intelligent grounds, of which they are conscious, are India and Japan. In China also there are no doubt large bodies of literati, but as a class they have not yet come into the modern world and into contact with Christianity. Even down to the Boxer rising of 1900, the wall of conservative patriotism shut off the literati in China from the outer civilisation and religions.

Indians themselves to be our witnesses.

Fortunately for students of India, her new literati are not merely in touch with the modern world, but express their minds readily in public meetings and in print. From themselves we shall chiefly quote in justifying the statements that will be made regarding the former or the modern religious opinions of India. To non-Christian or secular writers, also, we shall chiefly go, that the bias may rather be against than for the acknowledgment of change and progress. Our plan is to pronounce as little as possible upon either the Christian or the Hindu positions. We are observers of the religious ideas of modern India, and desire our readers to come into touch with modern Indians and to see for themselves.

Obstacles to changes in religion.

Education strips new Indians of belief.

Truth is great and will prevail, but let us not under-estimate the difficulties in the way of new opinions in India, where these do not appeal to the natural desires for power or status or comfort. I have already referred to the deep-rooted notion that Hinduism is of the soil of India, and adherence to it bound up with the national honour. I refer to it here again only to glance at a kindred notion, common among Anglo-Indians, that the Indian religion is the outcome of Indian environment, and is "consequently" the best religion for India. That superficial fallacy, undoubtedly, alienates the sympathy of many Anglo-Indians from religious and social progress in India. Thrice at least did one of the most distinguished viceroys, when addressing native audiences, advise them to stick to their own beliefs, using these or very similar words. He was addressing Mahomedans at one place, Hindus at the second place, and Buddhists at the third, and we leave his advice at one place to contradict his advice at another. Certainly let us allow for variation in local usage, and in subjective opinion, while we are insisting on the universality and objectivity of truth. For in spite of new and strange environment, in spite of that prevailing notion that religion is a racial thing, of the natural disinclination to change, of modern agnosticism and materialism when the old ideas do give way—in spite of these things, some of the cardinal features of Christianity are commending themselves to educated India. Far from religion being racial, the recent religious evolution of India suggests that in respect of the religious instinct and the religious faculty, mankind are one, not divided. *A priori*, therefore, we might anticipate that the elements of Christianity which have proved dynamical with new India will be the same that have proved their dynamic with educated men at home. So far as the situation in India has been created by the destructive influence of modern education, and by what may be called the modern spirit, the same influences are telling both in Europe and in India; they have come from Europe to India. There is the same unwillingness to believe in the supernatural, and the same demand that religion shall satisfy ethical and utilitarian tests. One difference, however, we may note. The educated men of India may not be living so entirely in the modern atmosphere as the men of Europe and America; but in India the modern spirit finds usages and systems of thought more inconsistent with modern ideas. As a consequence, where in India the modern spirit *has* come, it has stripped men barer of belief. Listen to the following curious conglomeration, showing the influences at work, constructive and destructive. It is a passage from the pamphlet already referred to, *The Future of India*; the author is arguing for what he calls "practical recognition of the Fatherhood of God"—one new positive idea. That idea he takes to mean that "God is the Father of all nations and religions," and that *therefore* "it does not matter much to what religion a man belongs, so far as the future of his soul is concerned." Does not that signify that he himself is stripped bare of belief? From which modern notion, that religion does not matter much, he next argues that a man ought to deny himself the luxury and "satisfaction of breaking his religious fetters," *i.e.* of seceding from his own faith and joining another. He ought to stick to his community, says this writer, and "have the satisfaction of working for the elevation of his countrymen." There we have the new political consciousness. The writer, it should be added, says some plain things about the need of social reform.

---

Three dynamical elements of Christianity.

---

As proved by observation in India, the dynamical elements of Christianity may be briefly enumerated as follows. Monotheism, tending more and more to the distinctively Christian idea of God, Our Father, is commending itself, and being widely accepted. Secondly, in a remarkable degree, Jesus Christ Himself is being recognised and receiving general homage. In a less degree, and yet notably, the Christian conception of the Here and Hereafter is commending itself to the minds of the new-educated Hindus. In the new religious organisations also, the Christian manner of worship and of public worship commends itself almost as a matter of course. In none of these spheres am I describing the outcome of visible conflict or of any loud controversy. Rather, Christianity brought close to the religious instincts and the religious ideas of India has been like a great magnet introduced among a number of kindred but non-magnetised bodies lying loosely around. In the presence, simply, of these dynamical elements, or in contact with them, Indian religious thought is becoming polarised. Towards and away from the same great points, Indian religious thought is setting. These dynamical elements of Christianity, and the illustration of their power, will be considered in the following chapters.

  Of the elements of Christianity that have proved themselves dynamical, we may note the natural order in which they have come. The order in which I have stated them is the order in which they asserted themselves, first "God Our Father," then "Jesus Christ Himself." First, of this world in which we find ourselves, when our *minds* awake, we must have some satisfying conception. The belief in one God, in Him for whom we can find no better name than "Our Father," approved itself to awakened India, to the *intellectually* enlightened, and in the first place to small groups of enlightened men in the large towns, the centres of modern education and Christian influence. Then came an advance of a different nature altogether. To those spiritually minded and more intense men who needed a religious master, a hero, to whom their *hearts* might go out, there came, after certain obstacles had been broken down, some knowledge of the actual historical Jesus Christ. The first stage satisfied the *mind* of modern educated India; the second stage concerns the highest affections and the lives. We know the step, when in the Apostles' Creed we pass from "I believe in God the Father Almighty, Maker of heaven and earth," to the words "and in Jesus Christ." Thereat we have brought theology down from heaven to earth; or rather, in these days we would say, in Jesus Christ we have obtained on earth, in actual history, in our affections, a foundation on which to rear our system of actual and motive-giving belief.

# CHAPTER X

## THE NEW RELIGIOUS ORGANISATIONS OF INDIA IN THE NINETEENTH CENTURY

### THE INDIAN CHRISTIAN CHURCH AND THE BRĀHMAS

Children of one family.

Two physical changes on the face of a country.

When we consider how the face of a country has been altered during the lapse of time, two great changes may be noticed, both of them due to the action of man. First we may observe that the whole general character of the country has undergone transformation. Gone are the ancient forests of Scotland, which of old in many districts clad the whole countryside, and with them have gone the wild animals which they sheltered. The forests destroyed, and the rainfall in consequence less abundant, the surface marshes and lakes have in many places vanished, taking the old agues and fevers in their train. Instead of the strongholds of chieftains in their fastnesses, surrounded by bands of their clansmen and retainers, has come the sober, peaceful, life of independent tenants, agricultural or artisan. And so on, down through the general changes wrought on the face of a land by modern conditions of life, we might watch the evolution of new features of the landscape. But we turn to the other kind of change, which is more noticeable at first sight, and is more directly due to the action of man. Great, laboriously cultivated, fields now stretch where formerly there was only waste or forest, or at best small sparsely scattered patches; and the very products of the soil in these new spacious fields are in many cases new. Where, for example, even in Britain before the close of the seventeenth century, were the great fields of potatoes and turnips and red clover, and even of wheat, which now meet the eye everywhere as the seasons return? Where in India before the British period were the vast areas now under tea and coffee, jute and cotton, although the two last have been grown and manufactured in India from time immemorial? "It might almost be said that, from Calcutta to Lahore, 50 per cent. of the prevalent vegetation, cultivated and wild, has been imported into India within historic times."[51]

All that, of course, is a parable. Likewise, in the new India we are studying, product of new modern influences direct and indirect, two kinds of religious changes impress us. There is, first, the gradual change coming over the whole thought of the people, a transformation like that wrought upon the face and climate of many lands. There is, further, the religious change, more immediately evident, in the new Indian religious organisations of the past century, analogous to the new, cultivated, products of the soil.

As change more definite and perceptible, we look first at the new Indian religious organisations. Within the British period, four organised religious movements attract our notice. They are: I. The new Indian Christian Church; II. The Brāhma Samāj and the kindred Prārthanā Samājes; III. The Ārya Samāj; and IV. The Theosophical Society, which in India now stands for the revival of Hinduism.

I. To hear the native Indian Church reckoned among the products of the British period may be surprising to some. There are indeed Christian communities in India older than the Christianity of many districts in Britain, and even excluding the Syrian and Roman Christians of India we must acknowledge that the Protestant Christian community dates farther back than the British period. Yet in a real sense the Protestant Indian Church, and the progressive character of the whole Indian Church, belong to the century just closed. The Moravians and one English Missionary Society excepted, all the great Missionary Societies now at work have come into being since 1793. In 1901 the native *Protestant* community in India, outcome of these Societies' labours, numbered close upon a million souls.

The Indian Christian Church is a living organisation, or congeries of organisations, over two and a half million souls all told, and growing rapidly. The exact figures in 1901 were 2,664,313, showing an increase during ten years of 30.8 per cent. The figures exclude Eurasians and Europeans; and in Anglo-Indian speech, we may remark, all Americans and Australians and South African whites and the like are Europeans. The attitude of the Indian Christian Church to the new ideas introduced by the British connection and by the modern world can readily be understood. Cut off, cast off, by their fellow-countrymen, and brought into closer contact than any others with Europeans in their missionaries and teachers, their minds have been open to all the new ideas. We know in fact that Indian Christians are often charged, by persons who do not appreciate the situation, with being over-Europeanised. It may be so in certain ways, but, irrespective of Christianity or Hinduism, the adoption of European ways results from contact with Europeans, and in certain respects is almost a condition of intercourse with Europeans. Let those, for example, who talk glibly about Indians sticking to their own dress, know that gentlemen in actual native dress are not allowed to walk on that side of the bandstand promenade in Calcutta where Europeans sit—a scandal crying for removal. With regard to the new national consciousness, it may be repeated that the Indian Christian community is almost as alive with the national feeling as the educated Hindu community. As the Indian Church becomes at once more indigenous and more thoroughly educated in Western learning, as it becomes less identified with European denominations, and less dependent upon stimulus from without, it will no doubt become still more national in every sense, be more recognised as one of India's institutions, and become a powerful educator in India. Once within the environment of the national feeling, the seed of Christian thought and modern ideas will spring up and spontaneously flourish. The future progress of the Indian Church may be said to depend upon the growth of that national consciousness within it. The sense of independence and the duty of self-support and union are, properly, being fostered in the native churches. But one of the dangers ahead undoubtedly is that, like one of the other religious movements of the past century, or like the Ethiopian Church in South Africa, the Indian Church may become infected with the political rather than the religious aspect of the idea.

---

The Brāhma Samāj.

---

Rammohan Roy.

---

II. *The Brāhma Samāj.*—Next to the Christian Church in order of birth of the issue of the new age, comes the Brāhma Samāj or Theistic Association. It was founded in Calcutta in 1828 by the famous reformer, Raja Rammohan Roy, first of modern Indians. The Brāhma Samāj is confessedly the outcome of contact with Christian ideas. By the best known of the Brāhma community, the late Keshub Chunder Sen, it was described as "the legitimate offspring of the wedlock of Christianity with the faith of the

Hindu Aryans." "No other reformation" [in India], says the late Sir M. Monier Williams, "has resulted in the same way from the influence of European education and Christian ideas." The founder himself, Raja Rammohan Roy, was indeed more a Christian than anything else, although he wore his brahman thread to the day of his death in order to retain the succession to his property for his son. In London and in Bristol, where he died in 1833, he associated himself with Dr. Carpenter and the more orthodox section of the Unitarians, explicitly avowing his belief in the miracles of Christ generally, and particularly in the resurrection. In Calcutta, indeed, the origin of the Brāhma Samāj was acknowledged at its commencement. After attending the Scotch and other Churches in Calcutta, and then the Unitarian Church, Rammohan Roy and his native friends set up a Church of their own, and one name for it among educated natives was simply the Hindu Unitarian Church. It is a secondary matter that, to begin with, the reformer believed that he had found his monotheism in the Hindu Scriptures, now known to all students as the special Scriptures of pantheism.

Raja Rammohan Roy, the brave man who made a voyage to Britain in defiance of caste, the champion of the widow who had often been virtually obliged to lay herself on her dead husband's pyre, the strenuous advocate of English education for Indians, the supporter of the claim of Indians to a larger employment in the public service, has not yet received from New India the recognition and honour which he deserves. To every girl, at least in Bengal, the province of widow-burning, he ought to be a hero as the first great Indian knight who rode out to deliver the widows from the torturing fire of Suttee.

Service of the Brāhma Samāj to India.

As its theistic name implies, the Brāhma Samāj professedly represents a movement towards theism, *i.e.* a rise from the polytheism and idolatry of the masses and a rejection of the pantheism of Hindu philosophy. Of course, noteworthy though it be, the foundation of the Brāhma Samāj in 1828 was not the introduction of monotheism to India. In the Indian Christian Church and in Mahomedanism, the doctrine of one, personal, God had been set forth to India, and in one of the ancient Hindu philosophical systems, the Yoga Philosophy, the same doctrine is implied. But in India, Christianity and Mahomedanism were associated with hostile camps; the Yoga Philosophy was known only to a few Sanscrit scholars. In Brāhmaism, the doctrine of one personal God became again natural naturalised in India. That has been its special service to India, to naturalise monotheism and many social and religious movements. For in India, things new and foreign lie under a peculiar suspicion. In the social sphere, the Brāhma Samāj repudiates caste and gives to women a position in society. As Indian *theists* also, when their first church was opened in 1830, they gave the Indian sanction to congregational worship and prayer, "before unknown to Hindus." For, the brahman interposing between God and the ignorant multitude, the Hindu multitude do not assemble themselves for united prayer, as Christians and Mahomedans do; and at the other end of the Hindu scale, the professed pantheist as such cannot pray. In proof of the latter statement, we recall the words of Swami Vivekananda, representative of Hinduism in the Parliament of Religions at Chicago in 1893, in a lecture "The Real and the Apparent Man," published in 1896. "It is the greatest of all lies," he writes somewhat baldly, although one is often grateful for a bald, definite statement, "that we are mere men; we are the God of the Universe.... The worst lie that you ever told yourself is that you were born a sinner.... The wicked see this universe as a hell, and the partially good see it as heaven, and the perfect beings realise it as God Himself.... By mistake we think that we are impure, that we are limited, that we are separate. The real man is the One Unit Existence." Prayer is therefore irrational for a pantheist, for no man is separate from God.

## Its limited membership.

The influence of the Brāhma Samāj has been far greater than its numerical success. Reckoned by its small company of 4050 members,[52] some of them certainly men of the highest culture and of sincere devoutness, the Brāhma Samāj is a limited and local movement, limited largely to the province of Bengal, and even to a few of the larger towns in the province. But if the taint of the intellectual origin of the Brāhma Samāj be still visible in the eclecticism that it professes, in its rejection of the supernatural, and in its poor numerical progress, it has nevertheless done great things for India.

## The Brāhma Samāj and the national feeling.

As yet the Brāhma Samāj has remained unaffected by the political aspect of the new national feeling. Early in its history there was, indeed, a section of the Samāj resolved to limit the selection of scriptures to the scriptures of the Hindus, but the late Keshub Chunder Sen successfully asserted the freedom of the Samāj, and probably saved it from the narrow patriotic groove and from the political character of the third of the new religious organisations, the Ārya Samāj.

## Prārthanā Samājes or Prayer Associations of S.W. India.

*The Prārthanā Samājes* or Prayer Associations of South-Western India.—
The history of India is pre-eminently the history of Northern India, that is
of the great plains of the Ganges and the Punjab. One may test it by the
simple academical test of reckoning what percentage of marks in an
examination on Indian history is assigned to the events of the great
northern plains. It is the same in the more recent religious history of India.
The southern provinces of Bombay and Madras have contributed very little
in respect of new religious life, organised or unorganised, compared with
the northern provinces of Bengal, the United Provinces, and the Punjab.
The Prārthanā Samājes or Prayer Associations of Bombay and South-
western India are monotheistic like the Brāhma Samāj, and have their halls
for their own worship. But socially they have not severed themselves from
their Hindu brethren, and do not figure in the Census as separate. Even
compared with the Brāhma Samāj, they are few in number. The first
Prārthanā Samāj was founded in Bombay in 1867. In Madras there is a
small representation of the Brāhma Samāj.

# CHAPTER XI

## NEW RELIGIOUS ORGANISATIONS

## THE ĀRYAS AND THE THEOSOPHISTS.

"Let us receive not only the revelations of the past, but also welcome joyfully the revelations of the present day."

—BISHOP COLENSO.

The Ārya Samāj.

III. *The Ārya Samāj* or *Vedic Theistic Association*—In contrast to the Samājes which are leavening the country but themselves are numerically unprogressive, are two other organisations—first, the Ārya Samāj of the United Provinces and the Punjab, and secondly, the Theosophists, who are now most active in Upper India, with Benares the metropolis of Hinduism, as their headquarters. These two have taken hold of educated India as no other movements yet have done. They appeal directly to patriotic pride and the new national feeling, or, more truly, are primarily shaped thereby.

Founded in 1875, the Āryas are the most rapidly increasing of the new Indian sects. In 1901 they numbered 92,419, an increase in the decade of 131 per cent. What ideas have such an attraction for the educated middle class, for to that class the Āryas almost exclusively belong? In certain parts of the United Provinces and the Punjab, it seems as much a matter of course that one who has received a modern education should be an Ārya, as that in certain other provinces he should be a supporter of the Congress.

Foundation ideas of the Āryas—two.

The prime motive ideas are two. One is the result of modern education and of Christian influence, namely, a consciousness that in certain grosser aspects, such as polytheism, idolatry, animal sacrifices, caste, and the seclusion of women, the present-day Hinduism cannot be defended. Those things the Āryas repudiate,—all honour to them for their protest in behalf of reason, although in respect of caste and the seclusion of women, their theory is said to be considerably ahead of their practice. In the same modern spirit every Ārya member pledges himself to endeavour to diffuse knowledge; and a college and a number of schools are carried on by Āryas in the Punjab. Repudiating all those current customs, of course the Āryas have parted company with the orthodox Hindus. Ārya preachers denounce the corruptions of Hinduism, and in turn, what may be called a Great Council of orthodox Hindus has pronounced condemnation on the Āryas. At an assembly of about four hundred Hindu pandits, held in 1881 in the Senate House of the University in Calcutta, the views of the founder of the Āryas, Dyanand Saraswati, were condemned as heterodox.[53]

The second motive idea is the new national consciousness, the new patriotic feeling of Indians. The patriotic feeling is manifest in the name; the Āryas identify themselves with the Āryans, the Indo-European invaders of India, from whom the higher castes of Hindus claim to be descended. Virtually, we may say, the Āryas claim by their name to be the pure original Hindus.

Infallibility of the Vedas the leading tenet at first.

To the first influence we may assign one of the chief doctrines of the Āryas, namely, their monotheism. Others of their doctrines belong to the theology and philosophy of Hinduism, e.g. the ancient doctrine of the transmigration of souls, and the doctrine of the three eternal entities, God, the Soul, and Matter, the doctrinal significance of which we shall have occasion to consider hereafter. These three uncreated existences constitute one of the doctrines of the Joga system of Hindu philosophy. To the second, or patriotic, influence, we may assign especially the fundamental tenet of the founder of the Āryas, namely, the infallibility of the original Scriptures, the four Vedas, given, as he alleged, to Indian sages at the creation of the world. "Back to the Vedas!" we may say, is the cry of the Āryas. In effect, the cry is tantamount to the plea that the errors of Hinduism are only later accretions; and be it acknowledged that no sanction can be drawn from the Vedas for the prohibition of widow marriages, for the general prevalence of child marriages, for the tyranny of caste, for idolatry and several other objectionable customs.[54] Among the Āryas, therefore, we have the championship of things Indian in its crudest form. Ludicrous are the attempts to rationalise all the statements of the Vedas, and to find in them all modern science and modern ideas, pouring new wine into old wine-skins, in perfect innocence of "the higher criticism." Thus while animal sacrifices are proscribed by the Āryas, they are everywhere assumed in the Vedas, and two of the hymns in the Rigveda are for use at the sacrifice of a horse (a[s']wamedha).[55] According to an Ārya commentator, however, a[s']wamedha is to be translated not "sacrifice of a horse," but destruction of ignorance,—sacrifice of an ass, as one may jestingly say.[56] Offerings for deceased parents, prescribed in detail in the Vedas, are similarly rationalised into kind treatment of parents in old age. The ancient and modern condemnation of eating beef was rationalised by the Āryas as follows: To kill a cow is as bad as to kill many men. For suppose a cow to have a lifetime of fourteen or fifteen years. Her calves, let us say, would be six cow calves and six bull calves. The milk of the cow and her six cow calves during her natural lifetime would give food for a day to an army of 154,440 men, according to the calculation of the founder of the Āryas, while the labour of the other six calves as oxen would give a full meal to an army of 256,000 men. Therefore to kill a cow, etc., Q.E.D. Modern democracy, the Copernican system of astronomy, a knowledge of the American continent, of steamships, and of the telegraph are all discovered by Dyanand in the Vedas, as no doubt wireless telegraphy and radium would have been, had death not cut short, in 1883, the discoveries of the founder of the Āryas.[57]

The modern leaven still affecting the Āryas.

These specimens of Ārya exposition of the Vedas I have given with no intention of scoffing, although we may be permitted a laugh. I desire to show the conflict of modern ideas and the new patriotic feeling, and how the latter has affected the religious and theological position of the Āryas. It is the prominence of the patriotic feeling in many branches of the Samāj that has led some observers to describe it as less of a religious than a political organisation, anti-British and anti-Mahomedan and anti-Christian. But the opponents of the Samāj are always associated by Āryas with rival religions; *keranis, kuranis,* and *puranis* is their echoing list of their opponents,—namely, Christians *(kerani* being a corruption of *Christiani),* and believers in the Koran, and believers in the Purans, *i.e.* the later Hindu books. And that there is much more than political feeling is apparent in their latest developments. The leaven of modern ideas has now led to the rise of a party among the Āryas which is prepared to stand by reason out and out, and repudiate the founder's bondage to the Vedas and his *à priori* expositions. Popularly, the new party is known as the "flesh-eaters." At present the Samāj is about equally divided, but the more rationalistic section comprises most of the new-educated members. Should the Ārya Samāj retain, as their chief doctrinal positions, the perfection of pure original Hinduism and opposition to every other ism, no great foresight or historical knowledge is required to predict for the Āryas, despite their vigour, a speedy lapse from their reforming zeal into the position simply of a new Hindu caste, reverting gradually to type. Their fate is still in the balance.

## The Bombay Ārya Samāj.

The Ārya Samāj in Bombay does not repudiate caste. One of their principles is that no member is expected to violate any of his own special caste rules. Why, one cannot help asking, this invertebrate character of the new Indian religious associations in Western India? It is patent that what the Prārthanā Samājes of Western India are to the Brāhma Samāj of Bengal, the Ārya Samāj in Bombay is to that in the Punjab and the United Provinces—only feeble echoes. Bombay Indians lead their countrymen in commercial enterprise, and in political questions they take as keen an interest as any of the Indian races. With hesitation and with apologies to Parsee friends, we ask whether it is the numerous Parsees in Bombay who have made their fellow-westerns only worldly-wise. For to great commercial enterprise, the Parsees add a stubborn conservatism in religion.

## The Theosophical Society and the national feeling.

IV. *The Theosophists* are the only other new religious organisation whom we can notice.—Them too the new patriotic feeling has very largely shaped. Founded in America in 1875, the very year in which the Ārya Samāj was established in Bombay, the Theosophical Society professed to be "the nucleus of a Universal Brotherhood of Humanity," representing and excluding no religious creed and interfering with no man's caste. On the other hand, somewhat inconsistently, it professed to be a society to promote the study of Āryan and other Eastern literature, religion, and sciences, and to vindicate their importance; and it appealed for support, amongst others, "to all who loved India and would see a revival of her ancient glories, intellectual and spiritual." At the same time the society professed "to investigate the hidden mysteries of nature and the psychical powers latent in man." The society naturally gravitated towards India, and by 1884 had 87 branches in India and Ceylon, against 12 in all the rest of the world. Its career might easily have been predicted. Inevitably, when transplanted to India, about the year 1878, such a society came under the spell of the new national consciousness already referred to. For a time Theosophy shared with the political Congress the first place in the interest of New India, and crowds of educated Indians still assemble whenever Mrs. Besant, now the leading Theosophist, is to speak. One of the rules of the society, however, saved it from the descent into politics that has overtaken the Ārya Samāj and tainted it as a religious movement. Rule XVI (1884) forbids members, as such, to interfere in politics, and declares expulsion to be the penalty for violation of the rule.

## Ārya period of the Theosophical Society.

Consistently enough, when the society was transplanted to India, it entered into partnership with the Ārya Samāj; for two years, indeed, Madame Blavatsky, the first leader of the Theosophists, had been corresponding from America with the founder of the Āryas. The Ārya tenet of the infallibility of the original Hindu Scriptures needed no reconciliation with the Theosophist declaration of the ancient spiritual glories of India. But the Āryas are also religious reformers, while, as enlightened Hindus now complain, the Theosophists are more Hindu than the Hindus. After three years, in 1881, difference arose on the question of the personality of God. The Āryas, we have seen, are monotheist; the Theosophical Society, we shall see, is identified with brahmanical pantheism.[58]

## Buddhist period of the Theosophical Society.

## Pro-Hindu period of the Theosophical Society.

The Buddhist period of the Theosophical Society, which came next, is best known to general readers, but is only an episode in its history. In the early "eighties," we find the society pro-Buddhist, and apparently identifying *Buddhism* with "the ancient glories of India, spiritual and intellectual," that the society was professedly desirous to revive. We associate the period with the publication of *Esoteric Buddhism*, by Mr. A.P. Sinnett, one of the society's leaders, and with Madame Blavatsky's claim to be in spiritual communication with Mahatmas [great spirits] in Thibet, the Buddhist land, now robbed of its mystery by the British expedition of 1904. Madame Blavatsky claimed to be receiving letters carried straight from Thibet by some air-borne Ariel. The discovery in 1884 of Madame Blavatsky's trickery ended the exhibition of "psychical powers," and also apparently the Buddhist period of the society. That the society itself survived the exposure is proof that it had a deeper root than any mere cult of Buddhism or Spiritualism could give. Its appeal, as we have said, was to the new patriotic feeling in the sphere of religion. To Madame Blavatsky succeeded Mrs. Besant as leading spirit, and to the cult of Buddhism again succeeded the glorification of ancient Hinduism and now also apologies of Hinduism as it is; and to Madras as chief centre of Theosophy succeeded Benares, metropolis of Hinduism. Mrs. Besant proclaimed herself the reincarnation of some ancient Hindu pandit, and called upon Hindus to devote themselves to the study of the Sacred Sanscrit. Supported by many well-to-do Hindus, in 1900 she founded a college at Benares in which Hinduism might be lived and inculcated as Christianity is inculcated in the Indian Missionary Colleges. In the beginning of 1904 a great figure of the goddess Saraswati, the Hindu goddess of Learning, was being erected in the grounds of the College. The subordination of the Indian Theosophical Society, at least in the person of Mrs. Besant, to the pro-Hindu national movement may be pronounced complete. In the sphere of religion, this new Indian consciousness which has enveloped the Theosophists is a force opposed to change and reform. The Theosophical Society, which at the outset professed to be the nucleus of a Universal Brotherhood, is now fostering caste and Hindu exclusiveness, the antitheses of the idea of humanity. Yet, as we shall see, even in the text-books of Hindu Religion prepared for use in the Hindu College, Benares, Christian thought is not difficult to discover. And its meed of praise must not be withheld from the attempts of Theosophists and the Hindu College, Benares, to rationalise current Hindu customs and to reduce the chaos of Hindu beliefs to some system that will satisfy New India. Fain would the Theosophists propound, as we have already noted in the chapter, "New Social Ideas," that caste should be determined by character and occupation, not by birth. That being impossible, they would fain see the myriad of castes reduced to the original four named in Manu. To quote again the summing up regarding the caste system in the chief Hindu text-book referred to—"Unless the abuses which are interwoven with caste can be eliminated, its doom is certain." That is much from the leaders of the Hindu reaction. In Hinduism they may often see only what they wish to see, but they are not wholly blinded.

The Theosophists, it should be noted, do not figure as such in the Census. Indian Christians, Brahmas, and Āryas have all taken up a definite new position in respect of religion, and ticket themselves as such; the Theosophists are now at least mainly the apologists of things as they are, and require no name to differentiate themselves.

# CHAPTER XII

## THE NEW MAHOMEDANS

The Mahomedans, the other great religious community of India,[59] have been far less stirred by the new era than the Hindus, whom hitherto we have been chiefly considering. Only a small number of Mahomedans belong to the professional class, so that modern education and the awakening have not reached Mahomedans in the same degree as Hindus. Quite outnumbered also by Hindus, they identify themselves politically with the British rather than with the Hindus, so that as a body they do not support the Congress, the great Indian Political Association, and have no anti-British consciousness. Mahomedan solidarity is strong enough, but it is religious not national, and so it is only in the religious sphere that we find the new era telling upon Mahomedans. Two small religious movements may be noted curiously parallel to the Ārya and Brāhma movements among Hindus, and suggesting the operation of like influences.

As the Āryas preach a return to the pure original Hinduism of the Vedas, the first Mahomedan movement inculcates a return to the pure original Mahomedanism of the Koran. In particular, it urges a casting off of the Hindu customs and superstitions that the Indian converts to Mahomedanism have frequently retained,—the offerings to the dead, for example. In the first instance, the movement came from a seventeenth century Arabian sect, the Wahabbis, but the movement reached India only about the year 1820, and therefore is a feature of the period we are surveying. The movement belongs specially to Bengal and the United Provinces north-west of Bengal, and is known by a variety of local names, Wahabbi and other. Significant, as supporting what has been said regarding the absence of anti-British feeling among present-day Mahomedans, is the fact that in the first stages of the Wahabbi movement, both in Eastern and Western Bengal, the duty of war upon infidels—on the British and the Hindus in this case—was a prominent doctrine of the crusade. In

Mahomedan language, India was *Daru-l-harb* or a Mansion of War. In these later years, on the contrary, it is generally recognised by Mahomedans that India under the British rule is not *Daru-l-harb*, but *Daru-l-Islam*, or a Mansion of Islamism, in which war on infidels is not incumbent.[60] It may be noted that the decree, recently issued from Mecca, that British territory is Daru-l-Islam, can only refer to India.

---

The Aligarh movement analogous to Brahmaism.

---

Exactly like the Brahmas, the other new Mahomedan sect, in the modern rational spirit, have refined away their faith to a theism or deism purged of the supernatural. Mahomed's inspiration and miracles are rejected. These represent the modern rationalising spirit in religion; reason is their standard, and "reason alone is a sufficient guide." According to Sir Syed Ahmad, founder of the movement, "Islam is Nature, and Nature Islam." Hence the sect is sometimes called the Naturis,[61] or followers of *Natural* Religion, the adoption of the English word identifying them again with the Brāhmas, who are essentially the outcome of English education and Christian influence among Hindus. The Naturis, the modernised Mahomedans, have as their headquarters the Mahomedan Anglo-Oriental College at Aligarh in the United Provinces. It ought to be said that they also claim to be going back to pure original Mahomedanism before it was corrupted by the "Fathers" of Islam.

# CHAPTER XIII

## HINDU DOCTRINES—HOW THEY CHANGE

"As men's minds receive new ideas, laying aside the old and effete, the world advances. Society rests upon them; mighty revolutions spring from them; institutions crumble before their onward march."

*—Extract from Mr. Kiddle, an American writer, which occurs in a letter "received" by Madame Blavatsky from Koot Humi in Thibet.*

----

Will the new religious organisations survive?

----

The four new religious organisations described in the preceding chapters may or may not survive—who can tell? What would they become, or what would become of them, in the event, say, of the great nations of Europe issuing from some deadly conflict so balanced that India and the East had to be let alone, entirely cut off? The Indian Christian Church, hardly yet acclimatised so far as it is the creation of modern efforts, would she survive? The English sweet-pea, sown in India, produced its flowers, but not at first any vigorous self-propagating seed. The Brāhma Samāj, graft of West on East, and still sterile as an intellectual coterie, how would it fare, cut off from its Western nurture? The Ārya Samāj—what, in that event, would be her resistance to the centripetal force that we have noted in her blind patriotism? The reactionary Theosophists—after the provocative action had ceased—what of them? Would not the Indian jungle, which they are trying to reduce to a well-ordered garden of indigenous fruits, speedily lapse to jungle again? We shall not attempt to answer our own questions directly, but proceed to the second part of our programme sketched on p. 122. How far then have Christian and modern religious ideas been *naturalised* in New India, whether within the new religious organisations or without? Whatever the fate of the organisations, these naturalised ideas might be expected to survive.

----

Modification of doctrines.

----

We recall the statements made on ample authority in an earlier chapter, that certain aspects of Christianity are attracting attention in India and proving themselves possessed of inherent force and attractiveness. These, the dynamical elements of Christianity, were specially the idea of God the Father, the person of Jesus Christ, and the Christian conception of the Here and Hereafter. For although Hinduism declares a social boycott against any Hindu who transports his person over the sea to Europe, within India itself the Hindu mind is in close contact with such modern religious ideas. The wall built round the garden will not shut out the crows. Indeed, like the ancient Athenian, the modern Hindu takes the keenest interest in new religious ideas.

To comprehend the impression that such new religious ideas are making, we must realise in some measure the background upon which they are cast, both that part of it which the new ideas are superseding and the remainder which constitutes their new setting and gives them their significance. In brief, what is the present position of India in regard to religious belief; and in particular, what are the prevailing beliefs about God?

----------------------------------------------------
Indian beliefs about God—Polytheists; Theists; Pantheists.
----------------------------------------------------

A rough classification of the theological belief of the Hindus of the present day would be—the multitude are polytheists; the new-educated are monotheists; the brahmanically educated are professed pantheists. Rough as it is, we must keep the classification before us in trying to estimate the influence upon the Indian mind of the Christian idea of God. From that fundamental classification let us try to understand the Hindu position more fully.

----------------------------------------------------
No one doctrine is distinctive of Hinduism.
----------------------------------------------------

Let it be realised, in the first place, how *undefined* is the Hindu's religious position. From the rudest polytheism up to pantheism, and even to an atheistic philosophy, all is within the Hindu pale, like fantastic cloud shapes and vague mist and empty ether, all within the same sky. To the student of Hinduism, then, the first fact that emerges is that there are no distinctive Hindu doctrines. No one doctrine is distinctive of Hinduism. There is no canonical book, nowhere any stated body of doctrine that might be called the Hindu creed. The only common measure of Hindus is that they employ brahmans in their religious ceremonies, and even that does not hold universally. A saying of their own is, "On two main points all sects agree—the sanctity of the cow and the depravity of women." In contrast to Hindus in this respect of the absence of a standard creed, Mahomedans call themselves *kitabi* or possessing a book, since in the Koran they do possess such a canon. In the words of Mahomed, Christians and Jews likewise are "the peoples of the book," and have a defined theological position. But regarding Hindus, again, we note there is no doctrinal pale, no orthodoxy or heterodoxy. "We Europeans," writes Sir Alfred Lyall regarding Hinduism, "can scarcely comprehend an ancient religion, still alive and powerful, which is a mere troubled sea without shore or visible horizon."[62] In these days of opportunist denunciation of creeds, the amorphous state of creedless Hinduism may be noted.

The experience of the late Dr. John Henry Barrows, President of the Parliament of Religions at Chicago in 1893, may be quoted in confirmation of the absence of a Hindu creed. After he had won the confidence of India's representatives as their host at Chicago, and had secured for them a unique audience there, being himself desirous to write on Hinduism, he wrote to over a hundred prominent Hindus requesting each to indicate what in his view were some of the leading tenets of Hinduism. He received only one reply.

> Pantheism, Maya, and Transmigration may be called Hindu doctrines.

No one doctrine is distinctive of Hinduism. It is an extreme misleading statement, nevertheless, to say as some Western writers have done, and at least one Hindu writer,[63] that Hinduism is not a religion at all, but only a social system. There are several doctrines to which a great many Hindus would at once conventionally subscribe, and these I venture to call Hindu doctrines. In theological conversations with Hindus, three doctrines very frequently show themselves as a theological background. These are, first, Pantheism; secondly, Transmigration and Final Absorption into Deity; and, thirdly, Maya, i.e. Delusion, or the Unreality of the phenomena of Sense and Consciousness. I find a recent pro-Hindu writer making virtually the same selection. In the ninth century, she writes, Sankarachargya, the great upholder of Pantheism, "took up and defined the [now] current catch-words—maya, karma [the doctrine of works, or of re-birth according to desert], reincarnation, and left the terminology of Hinduism what it is to-day."... "But," she also adds, "they are nowhere and in no sense regarded as essential."[64] Naturally, then, the inquiry that we have set ourselves to will at the same time be an inquiry how far Christian thought has affected these three main Hindu doctrines of Pantheism, Transmigration, and Maya.

Polytheism with Monotheism.

Nor is it to be imagined that the Hindu polytheism, theism, and pantheism are distinguishable religious strata. "Uniformity and consistency of creeds are inventions of the European mind," says a cynical writer already quoted. "Hinduism bristles with contradictions, inconsistencies, and surprises," says Sir M. Monier Williams. The common people are indeed polytheists, at different seasons of the year and on different social occasions worshipping different deities, male or female, and setting out to this or that shrine, as the touts of the rival shrines have persuaded them. Nevertheless, an intelligent member of the humbler ranks is always ready to acknowledge that there is really only one God, of whom the so-called gods are only variations in name. Or his theory may be that there is one supreme God, under whom the popular deities are only departmental heads; for the presence of the great central British Government in India is a standing suggestion of monotheism. The officer who drew up the *Report of the Census of India*, 1901 (p. 363) gives an instance of this commingling of monotheism and polytheism. "An orderly," he writes, "into whose belief I was inquiring, described the relation between the supreme God and the Devata [minor Gods] as that between an official and his orderlies, and another popular simile often used is that of the Government and the district officer."[65] The polytheism of the masses may thus blend with the theism which is the ordinary intellectual standpoint of the educated classes.

Monotheism with Polytheism.

Rising to the next stage, namely, the theism of the educated class—the blending of their theism with the polytheism of the masses is illustrated in the July number of the magazine of the Hindu College, Benares, the headquarters of the late Hindu revival and of the pantheistic philosophy. In answer to an inquirer's question—"Is there only one God?" the reply is, "There is one supreme Lord or Ishvara of the universe, and there are minor deities or devas who intelligently guide the various processes of nature in their different departments in willing obedience to Ishvara." The Hindu College, Benares, be it remembered, is primarily one of the modern colleges whence the modern new-Indians come.

Monotheism with Pantheism.

Again, the modern theism of the educated, in like manner, very readily passes into the pantheism of the philosophers and of those educated in Sanscrit, which I have described as part of the accepted Hindu orthodoxy. For, whatever its origin, an observer finds the pantheistic idea emerge all over educated India. The late Sir M. Monier Williams speaks of pantheism as a main root of the original Indo-Aryan creed, which has "branched out into an endless variety of polytheistic superstitions." Whether that be so, or whether, as is now more generally believed, the polytheism is the aboriginal Indian plant into which the pantheistic idea has been grafted as communities have become brahmanised, the pantheistic idea very readily presents itself to the mind of the educated Hindu. In any discussion regarding human responsibility the idea crops up that *all* is God, "There is One only, and no second." We can scarcely realise how readily it comes to the middle-class Hindu's lips that God is all, and that there can be no such thing as sin. The pantheists are thus no separate sect from the theists, any more than the theists are from the polytheists. The same man, if a member of the educated class, will be polytheist in his established domestic religion, theist in his personal standpoint and general profession, and probably a pantheist in a controversy regarding moral responsibility, or should he set himself to write about religion.

---
Illustration of polytheism, monotheism, and pantheism commingling.

---

Take a statement of the mingling of polytheism, monotheism, and pantheism from the extreme south of India, a thousand miles away from Benares. "Though those men all affirmed," we read, "that there is only one God, they admitted that they each worshipped several. They saw nothing inconsistent in this. Just as the air is in everything, so God is in everything, therefore in the various symbols. And as our king has diverse representative Viceroys and Governors to rule over his dominions in his name, so the Supreme has these subdeities, less in power and only existing by force of Himself, and He, being all pervasive, can be worshipped under their forms."[66]

---
Pure pantheism rare.

---

At the top of all is the pure pantheist, a believer in the illusion of the senses, and generally though not always an ascetic. For life is not worth living if it is merely an illusion, and the illusion must be dispelled, and the world of the senses renounced. If "father and brother, etc., have no actual entity," said the reformer Raja Rammohan Roy [1829] when combating pantheism, "they consequently deserve no real affection, and the sooner we escape from them and leave the world the better." So the pantheist is generally an ascetic cut off from the world to be consistent in his pantheism. Yet again, we repeat that such pure pantheists are very rare, and that "in India forms of pantheism, theism, and polytheism are ever interwoven with each other."[67]

To one familiar with India, such a medley is neither inconceivable nor improbable; the debatable question only is, what sufficient account of the cause thereof can be given. Why is it that Hindu doctrine has never set? Why this incongruity between doctrine and domestic practice? Why this double-mindedness in the same educated individual? Much might be said in the endeavour to account for these characteristic features of India, the despair of the Christian missionary. I confine myself to the bearing of the question upon the influence of Christian ideas, and particularly of Christian theism.

Fluidity of Hindu thought; rigidity of Hindu practice.

For the student of this special aspect of Hinduism a second pertinent fact here emerges, namely, that Hindu practice is much more established than Hindu doctrine. The unchangeableness of Hindu ritual is not a new idea; it is its bearing on doctrine that has not been clearly considered. There *is*, then, a distinctly recognised Hindu orthodoxy in manners and worship, at least for each Hindu community, while there is no orthodoxy in doctrine. The broad distinctive marks of Hindu practice, we may repeat, are the social usage of caste, and the employment of brahmans in religious ritual. With ideas, then, thus fluid and practice thus rigid, it will be easily understood that Christian and modern ideas have made much greater headway in India than Christian customs and modes of worship. The mind of educated India has been Christianised to a much greater extent than the religious or domestic practices have been. Perhaps it might be said that all down the centuries of Christian Church history, opinion has often been in advance of worship and the social code, that social and religious conventionalities have lagged behind belief. If so, it is the marked conservatism in ceremonial that is noteworthy in India. While Hindu beliefs are dissolving or dropping out of the mind, Hindu practices are successfully resisting the solvent influences or only slowly being transformed.

More progress towards Christian thought than Christian practice.

It is not too much to say that the educated Hindu does not regard a fixed creed as a part of his Hinduism, but rather boasts of the doctrinal comprehensiveness of his religion. He joyfully lives in a ferment of religious thought, surrendering to the doctrine of a satisfying teacher, but the idea of creed subscription, or a doctrinal stockade, is utterly foreign to his nature. For him the standards are the fixed social usages and the brahmanical ritual. Hear a Hindu himself on the matter, the historian of *Hindu Civilisation during British Rule* [i. 60]: "Hinduism has ever been and still is as liberal and tolerant in matters of religious belief as it is illiberal and intolerant in matters of social conduct." In a recent pamphlet[68] an Anglo-Indian civilian gives his evidence clearly, if too baldly, of the fixity of practice and the mobility of belief. "The educated Hindu," he writes, "has largely lost his belief in the old myths about the gods and goddesses of the Hindu pantheon, and has learned to smile at many of the superstitions of his uneducated countrymen. But Hinduism as a religion that tells a man not only what he shall eat, what he shall drink, and wherewithal he shall be clothed, but tells him how to perform innumerable acts that men of other nations never think have anything to do with religion at all, Hinduism as an intricate social code, stands largely unaffected by the flood of Western education that has been poured upon the country. He instances a brahman, one of his own subordinates, college-bred and English-speaking, who, when away from home with his superior officer, had to cook his food for himself, because the brahman servant he had with him was of a lower division than his own, and he could not afford to hire a man of his own status among brahmans."

---

Thought independent of act.

---

We ask again for the cause of this progress in thought and stagnation in practice. In India, creed and practice go their own way; thinking is independent of acting. Listen to the naive standpoint assumed in the Confession or Covenant of a Theistic Association established in Madras in 1864. We read in article 3 that the person being initiated makes this declaration: "In the meantime, I shall observe the ceremonies now in use, but only where indispensable. I shall go through such ceremonies, where they are not conformable to pure Theism, as mere matters of routine, destitute of all religious significance—as the lifeless remains of a superstition which has passed away." And again in article 4: "I shall never endeavour to deceive anyone as to my religious opinions." In the revision of 1871, both articles were dropped, but in the earlier form there was no attempt to disguise that thought was independent of act. The familiar figure of Buddha in meditation, seated cross-legged and motionless, with vacant introspective eyes, oblivious of the outer world, is a type of the separation of thought from act that seems natural to India or to the Indian mind, type also of the independence of each thinker. The thinker secludes himself; "the mind is its own place." To become a thinker signifies to become an ascetic recluse; even modern enlightenment often removes an Indian from fellow-feeling with his kind.

How is it so? I say nothing of the climate of tropical India as a contributory cause. The way in which Hindu learning was and is transmitted, is itself almost sufficient explanation of the independence and the fluidity of religious doctrine. Hinduism has no recognised Theological Faculties as training schools for the priesthood. *Buddhist* monasteries of the early Christian centuries we do read of, institutions corresponding to our universities, to which crowds of students resorted, and where many subjects were taught; but the *Hindu* lore is transmitted otherwise. Beside or in his humble dwelling, the learned Hindu pandit receives and teaches and shares his poverty with his four, five, or it may be twenty disciples, who are to be the depositaries of his lore, and in their turn its transmitters. Such an institution is a Sanscrit tol, where ten to twenty years of the formative period of a young pandit's life may be spent. Without printed books and libraries and intercourse with kindred minds, there may be as many schools of thought as there are teachers. And all this study, be it remembered, has no necessary connection with the priesthood. Tols have no necessary connection with temples, or temples with tols. Hereditary priests are independent of Theological Schools. Recently, indeed, in Bengal these tols have been taken up by the Education Department, and their studies are being directed to certain fixed subjects.

The twofold priesthood—religious teachers and celebrants.

How doctrine moves independently of ritual.

Another feature of the organisation of Hinduism, hitherto insufficiently noticed, has a still closer connection with this freedom of thought and fixity of practice. The Indian mind is open to new religious ideas, while the religious customs of India remain almost unaffected, *because* the priesthood of Hinduism is two-fold. One set of priests, called purohits, are merely the celebrants at worship and ceremonies; the second set, called gurus, theoretically more highly honoured, are or were the religious teachers of the people. Among Mahomedans there is a somewhat similar two-fold priesthood, although among them doctrine is not divorced from religious worship and ritual. But in Christianity we have not specialised so far. A Christian clergyman, as we know, holds both offices; he is both the religious teacher and the celebrant at sacraments, etc. In Hinduism, with these two sets of priests entirely separate, it is evident that a change may take place in the creed without the due performance of the Hindu ritual being affected. A striking instance of the divergence of guru from purohit is given by Sir Monier Williams in another connection. In India, he says, no temples are more common than those containing the symbol of the God Siva—there are said to be thirty million symbols of Siva scattered over India—yet among gurus there is scarcely one in a hundred whose vocation is to impart the mantra (the saving text) of Siva.[69] It has already been explained how the creed of Hinduism is dissolving while its practices remain; to restate the fact otherwise now—The hereditary purohits continue to be employed many times a year in a Hindu household, as worship, births, deaths, marriages, and social ceremonies recur, but the hereditary gurus as religious teachers have become practically defunct.[70] Literally, the *one* duty of a guru has come to be to communicate once in a lifetime to each Hindu his saving mantra or Sanscrit text; periodically thereafter, the guru may visit his clients to collect what dues they may be pleased to give. The place of religious teacher in Hinduism is vacant, and Christianity and modern thought are taking the vacant place. The modern middle-class Hindu is in need of a guru. For mere purohits, as such, he has a small and a declining reverence; but holy men, as such, his instinct is to honour—one of the pleasing features of Hinduism. We can understand it all when we remember how in the Christian Church, in a crisis like that from which the Church is now emerging, many come to be married by the clergyman who have practically lapsed from the faith.

# CHAPTER XIV

## THE NEW THEISM

"The idea of God is the productive and conservative principle
of civilisation; as is the religion of a community, so will be
in the main its morals, its laws, its general history."

*Vico* and *Michelet* (Prof. Flint's *Philosophy of History*).

Polytheism receding before Monotheism.

In some measure, then, we understand how Hindu polytheism, theism,
and pantheism are related to each other; we realise in some measure the
openness of the Indian mind, and we now ask ourselves how far the
Christian doctrine of God has impressed itself upon that open mind. Of
the polytheistic masses it has already been pointed out that intelligent
individuals will now readily acknowledge that there is truly one God only.
Further, that the polytheistic idolatry which is now associated with the
masses once extended far higher up the scale, is evident to anyone reading
the observations made early in the nineteenth century. Early travellers in
India, like the French traveller Tavernier of the seventeenth century, speak
of the Indians without distinction as idolaters, contrasting them with the
Mahomedans of India. In the *Calcutta Gazette* of 1816, Raja Rammohan
Roy, the learned opponent of Hindu idolatry, the Erasmus of the new era,
is called the *discoverer* of theism in the sacred books of the Hindus.
Rammohan Roy himself disclaimed the title, but writing in 1817, he speaks
of "the system of idolatry into which Hindus are now completely sunk."[71]
Many learned brahmans, he says in the same pamphlet, are perfectly aware
of the absurdity of idol worship, indicating that the knowledge belonged
only to the scholars. His own object, he said, was to declare *the unity* of God
as the real thought of the Hindu Scriptures. Across India, on the Bombay
side, we find clear evidence of the state of opinion among the middle class
in 1830, from the report of a public debate on the Christian and Hindu
religions. The antagonists were, on the one side, the Scottish missionary Dr.
John Wilson and others, and on the other side two leading officials of the
highest Government Appellate Court, men who would now rank as

eminent representatives of the educated class. One of these demanded proof that there was only one God.[72]

---

The beginning of the nineteenth century.

---

Monotheistic belief a broadening wedge between pantheism and polytheism.

---

Returning to Bengal, it would seem from Rammohan Roy's evidence that in 1820 the standpoint of the learned at that time was exactly what we have called the standpoint of an intelligent individual among the masses to-day, namely, a plea that the multitude of gods were agents of the one Supreme God. "Debased and despicable," he writes, "as is the belief of the Hindus in three hundred and thirty millions of gods, they (the learned) pretend to reconcile this persuasion with the doctrine of the unity of God, alleging that the three hundred and thirty millions of gods are subordinate agents assuming various offices and preserving the harmony of the universe under one Godhead, as innumerable rays issue from one sun."[73] Turning to testimony of a different kind, we find Macaulay speaking about the polytheistic idolatry he knew between 1834 and 1838. "The great majority of the population," he writes, "consists of idolaters." Macaulay's belief was that idolatry would not survive many years of English education, and we shall now take note how in the century the sphere of idolatry and polytheism has been limited. At the beginning of the nineteenth century, we may now say that Indian Hindu society consisted of a vast polytheistic mass with a very thin, an often invisible, film of pantheists on the top. The nineteenth century of enlightenment and contact with Christianity has seen the wide acceptance of the monotheistic conception by the new-educated India. The founding of the Brāhma Samāj or Theistic Association in 1828 by Rammohan Roy has already been called the commencement of an indigenous theistic church outside the transplanted theism of Indian Christianity and Indian Mahomedanism. Strictly rendered, the divine name *Brahmā*, adopted by the Brāhmas, expresses the pantheistic idea that God is the *One without a second*, not the theistic idea of one personal God; but what we are concerned with is, that it was in the monotheistic sense that Rammohan Roy adopted the term. To him Brahmā was a personal God, with whom men spoke in prayer and praise. As a matter of fact the pantheistic formula, "One only, no second," occurs in the creeds of all three new monotheistic bodies, Brāhmas, Prārthanā Samājists, and Āryas, but in the same monotheistic sense. The original Sanscrit of the formula (Ekam eva advityam), three words from the Chhāndogya Upanishad, is regularly intoned (droned) in the public worship of Brāhmas. Like a wedge between the polytheism of the masses below and the pantheism of the brahmanically educated above, there came in this naturalised theism, a body of opinion ever widening as modern education enlarges its domain. It is one of the *events* of Indian history. Now, pantheistic in argument and polytheistic in domestic practices as educated Hindus still are, they never call themselves pantheists, and would resent being called polytheists; they call themselves theists. "Every intelligent man is now a monotheist," writes the late Dr. John Murdoch of Madras, an experienced observer.[74] "Many" (of the educated Hindus), says a Hindu writer, "—I may say most of them—are in reality monotheists, but monotheists of a different type from those who belong to the Brāhma Samāj. They are, if we may so call them, passive monotheists.... The influence of the Hindu environment is as much perceptible in them as that of the Christian environment."[75] Professor Max Müller and Sir M. Monier Williams are of the same opinion. "The educated classes look with contempt upon idolatry.... A complete disintegration of ancient faiths is in progress in the upper strata of society. Most of the ablest thinkers become pure Theists or Unitarians."[76] That change took place within the nineteenth century, a testimony to the force of Christian theism in building up belief, and to the power of the modern Indian atmosphere to dissipate irrational and unpractical beliefs. For, in contact with the practical instincts of Europe, the pantheistic denial of one's own personality—a disbelief in one's own consciousness, the thought that there is no thinker—was bound to give way, as well as the irrational polytheism. Very unphilosophical may have been Lord Byron's attitude to the idealism of Berkeley: "When Bishop Berkeley said there was no matter, 'twas no matter what he said." But that represents the modern atmosphere which New India is breathing, and it is fatal to pantheism.

---

The spread of monotheism traced.

---

It is interesting to note how monotheism spread. The Brāhma Samāj of Madras was founded in 1864, theistic like the mother society, the Brāhma Samāj of Bengal. Three years later the first of similar bodies on the west side of India was founded, the Prārthanā Samājes or Prayer Associations of Bombay. Their very name, the *Prayer* Associations, implies the dual conception of God and Man, for the pantheistic conception does not admit of the idea of prayer any more than it admits of the other dualistic conceptions of revelation, of worship, and of sin. These movements, again, were followed in the United Provinces and the North-West of India by the founding of the *Ārya Samāj*, or, as I have called it, the Vedic Theistic Association, also professedly theistic. Polytheism and pantheism alike, the Āryas repudiate. For the gods and goddesses of the Hindu pantheon, the founder of the Āryas declared there was no recognition in the Vedas.

Demonstrable or not, that is the Ārya position. The rejection of pantheism by such a body is noteworthy, for pantheism is identified with India and the Vedanta, the most widely accepted of the six systems of Indian philosophy, and the Ārya Samāj is nothing if not patriotic. It is above all pro-Indian and pro-Vedic. Their direct repudiation of pantheism may not be apparent to Western minds. Āryas predicate three eternal entities, God, the Soul, and Matter,[77] and this declaration of the reality of the soul and of matter is a direct denial of the pantheistic conception, its very antithesis. One pantheistic formula is: "Brahma is reality, the world unreality" (Brahma satyam, jagan mithyā). The Pantheist must declare, and does declare in his doctrine of Maya or Delusion, that the soul and matter are illusions.

---

The progress of monotheism seen in the *Text-book of Hindu Religion.*

---

A very striking illustration of the present insufficiency of the pantheistic conception of God and of the movement of educated India towards theism is to be found where one would least expect it—in connection with the Hindu Revival. In 1903 an *Advanced Text-book of Hindu Religion and Ethics* was published by the Board of Trustees of the Hindu College, Benares, a body representing the movement for a revival of Hinduism. It was a heroic undertaking to reconcile, in the one Text-book, Vedic, philosophic, and popular Hinduism, to harmonise all the six schools of philosophy, to embrace all the aspects of modern Hinduism, and lastly to satisfy the monotheistic opinions of modern enlightened Hindus.

---

What is Pantheism?

---

To appreciate the testimony of the Text-book, we must enter more fully into the orthodox Hindu theological position. Pantheism, or the doctrine that God is all and all is God—what does it imply? Pantheism is a theory of creation, that God is all, that there are in truth no creatures, but only unreal phantasies appearing to darkened human minds, because darkened and half-blind. As such, its nearest Christian analogue would be the thought that in every phenomenon we have God's fiat and God's reason, and that "in Him we live and move and have our being." Pantheism is a theory of spiritual culture, that our individuality is ours only to merge it in His, although on this line, the Christian soon parts company with the Indian pantheistic devotee, who seeks to *merge* his consciousness in God, not to train himself into active sonship. Pantheism is a theory of God's omnipresence, and may be little more than enthusiastic feeling of God's omnipresence, such as we have in the 139th psalm, "Whither shall I go from Thy presence? and whither shall I flee from Thy spirit?" That Oriental mysticism and loyalty to an idea we can allow for. It is in that aspect that pantheism is in closest contact with the belief of the new educated Hindu. But in brahmanical philosophy, pantheism is nothing else than the inability to pass beyond the initial idea of infinite preexistent, unconditioned, Deity. To the pantheist, let us remember, there is Deity, but there are no real deities; there is a Godhead, but there are no real persons in the Godhead. In the view of the pantheist, when we see aught else divine or human than this all-embracing Deity or Godhead, it is only a self-created mist of the dim human eye, in which there play the flickering phantasms of deities and human individuals and things. "In the Absolute, there is no thou, nor I, nor God," said Ramkrishna, a great Hindu saint who died in 1886.[78] In Hindu phraseology, every conception other than this all-comprehending Deity is *Maya* or delusion, and salvation is "saving knowledge" of the delusion, and therefore deliverance from it. The perception of *manifoldness* is Maya or illusion, says a modern pro-Hindu writer. And again, "To India, all that exists is but a mighty curtain of appearances, tremulous now and again with breaths from the unseen that it conceals."[79]

---
Maya is implied in Pantheism.

---

---
The outcome of Maya.
---

The doctrine of Maya is, of course, a postulate, a necessity of Pantheism. Brahma is the name of the impersonal pantheistic deity. First among the unrealities, the outcome of Maya or Illusion or Ignorance, is the idea of a supreme *personal* God, Parameswar, from whom, or in whom, next come the three great personal deities, namely, the Hindu Triad, Brahmā (not Brahma), Vishnu, and Siva,—Creator, Preserver, and Destroyer respectively. These and all the other deities are the product of Maya, and thus belong to the realm of unreality along with Parameswar.[80] Popular theology, on the other hand, begins with the three great personal deities.

---
The Hindu Text-book transforms Pantheism into Monotheism.
---

Now come we again to the Text-book. Rightly, as scholars would agree, it describes the predominant philosophy of Hinduism as pantheistic. The Text-book, however, goes farther, and declares all the six systems of Hindu philosophy to be parts of one pantheistic system.[81] The word pantheism, I ought to say, does not occur in the Text-book. But here is its teaching. "All six systems," we are told, "are designed to lead man to the One Science, the One Wisdom which saw One Self Real and all else as Unreal." And again,

"Man learns to climb from the idea of himself as separate from Brahma to the thought that he is a part of Brahma that can unite with Him, and finally [to the thought] that he is and ever has been Brahma, veiled from himself by Avidyā" (that is, Ignorance or Maya). Our point is that the *Text-book of Hindu Religion* is professedly pantheistic, and the above is clearly pantheism and its postulate Maya. But in the final exposition of this pantheism, what do we find? To meet the modern thought of educated India, the pantheism is virtually given up.[82] Brahma, the One and the All, becomes simply *the Deity Unmanifested*; who shone forth to men as *the Deity Manifested*, Parameswar; of whom the Hindu Triad, Brahmā and Vishnu and Siva, are only three *names*. Maya or Delusion, the foundation postulate of pantheism, by which things *seem* to be,—by which the One seems to be many,—is identified with the creative will of Parameswar. In fact, Pantheism has been virtually transformed into Theism, Brahma into a Creator, and Maya into his creative and sustaining fiat. The *Text-book of the Hindu Religion* is finally monotheistic, as the times will have it.

> A Parsee claiming to be a monotheist.

As further confirmation of the change in the Indian mind, we may cite the paper read at the Congress on the History of Religions, Basel, 1904, by the Deputy High-priest of the Parsees, Bombay. The dualism of the Zoroastrian theology has hitherto been regarded as its distinctive feature, but the paper sought to show "that the religion of the Parsees was largely monotheistic, not dualistic."

The theistic standpoint of the younger members of the educated class of to-day is easily discoverable. The word *God* used in their English compositions or speeches, plainly implies a person. The commonplace of the anxious student is that the pass desired, the failure feared, is dependent upon the will of God—language manifestly not pantheistic. Religious expressions, we may remark, are natural to a Hindu.

> The conception of the Deity as female has gone from the minds of the educated.

In the new theism of educated Indians we may note that the conception of the deity as female is practically gone. Not so among the masses, particularly of the provinces of Bengal and Gujerat, the provinces distinctively of goddesses. The sight of a man in Calcutta in the first hour of his sore bereavement calling upon Mother Kali has left a deep impression upon me.[83] Be it remembered, however, what his cry meant, and what the name *Mother* in such cases means. It is a honorific form of address, not the symbol for devoted love. The *goddesses* of India, not the gods, are the deities to be particularly feared and to be propitiated with blood. It is energy, often destructive energy, not woman's tenderness that they represent, even according to Hindu philosophy and modern rationalisers. We may nevertheless well believe that contact with Christian ideas will yet soften and sweeten this title of the goddesses.

---

The new theism is largely Christian theism—God is termed Father;

---

Or Mother.

---

The new theism of educated India is more and more emphatically Christian theism. Anyone may observe that the name, other than "God," by which the Deity is almost universally named by educated Hindus is "The Father," or "Our Heavenly Father," or some such name. The new name is not a rendering of any of the vernacular names in use in modern India; it is due directly to its use in English literature and in Christian preaching and teaching. The late Keshub Chunder Sen's *Lectures in India*, addressed to Hindu audiences, abound in the use of the name. The fatherhood of God is in fact one of the articles of the Brāhma creed. In his last years, the Brahma leader, Keshub Chunder Sen, frequently spoke of God as the divine *Mother*, but we are not to suppose that it expresses a radical change of thought about God. Keshub Chunder Sen's last recorded prayer begins: "I have come, O Mother, into thy sanctuary"; his last, almost inarticulate, cries were: "Father," "Mother." Where modern Indian religious teachers address God as *Mother*, it is a modernism, an echo of the thought of the Fatherhood of God. The name is altered because the name of Mother better suits the ecstasies of Indian devotion, where the ecstatic mood is cultivated. A case in point is the Hindu devotee, Ramkrishna Paramhansa, who died near Calcutta in 1886. "Why," Ramkrishna Paramhansa asks, "does the God-lover find such pleasure in addressing the Deity as Mother? Because," his answer is, "the child is more free with its mother, and consequently she is dearer to the child than anyone else.[84] Another instance we find in the appeal issued by a committee of Hindu gentlemen for subscriptions towards the rebuilding of the temple at Kangra, destroyed by the earthquake of 1905. The president of the committee, signing the appeal, was a Hindu judge of the High Court at Lahore, a graduate from a Mission College. "There are Hindus," thus runs the appeal, "who by the grace of the Divine Mother could give the [whole] amount ... and not feel the poorer for it."[85]

The Ārya Samāj, on the other hand, seems set against speaking or thinking of God as the Father. Specially present to their minds and in their preaching is the thought of God's absolute justice; and they hold that His Justice and His Fatherhood are contradictory attributes. Virtue *will* have its reward, they assert, and Sin its punishment, both in this and the following existences. We recognise the working of their doctrine of transmigration, perhaps also the effect of a feeble presentation of the Christian doctrine of the Father's forgiveness of sin. Nevertheless, we may note in a hymn-book published in London for the use of members of the Ārya Samāj resident there, such hymns as "My God and Father, while I stray," and "My God, my Father, blissful name," as if the name were not explicitly excluded. We also read that the very last parting words of the founder of the Āryas himself were: "Let Thy will be done, O Father!"[86] The heart of man will not be denied the name and the feeling of "God who is our home." Turning again from the Āryas to the new citadel of Benares, and Hinduism, the Hindu College, Benares, we find that along with the Text-book already mentioned, there was published a *Catechism in Hindu Religion and Morals* for boys and girls. One question is, "Can we know that eternal Being (the "One only without a second," or "The All," *i.e.* pantheistic Deity)? The answer is, "Only when revealed as Ishwar, the Lord, the loving Father of all the worlds and of all the creatures who live in them." That idea of the loving Father, of divine Law and Love in one person, is new to Hinduism. The law of God may be only imperfectly apprehended, but the loving Fatherhood of God, the approachable one, has become manifest in India— one of Christianity's dynamic doctrines. Strangest confirmation of all, a Mahomedan preacher of Behar a few years ago was expounding from the Koran the Fatherhood of God. The name and thought of the divine Father established, we may leave name and thought to be invested with their full significance in the fulness of time.

"It is with Pantheism, not Polytheism, that a rising morality will have to reckon," says Sir Alfred Lyall.[87] The result of all our observation has been different. Pantheism is melting out of the sky of the educated, and if nothing else take its place, it will be a selfish materialism or agnosticism, not avowed or formulated yet shaping every motive, that the new morality will have to reckon with.

# CHAPTER XV

## JESUS CHRIST HIMSELF

"Tandem vicisti, Galilaee"

—said to have been uttered by Julian, the Apostate emperor.

---
Pantheism does not lead to belief in "the Son of God."
---

Pantheism, it has been said, lends itself to the lead to belief idea of avatars or incarnations of deity, and Hinduism, therefore, is familiar with avatars. Observation contradicts this *à priori* reasoning, nay, it justifies a statement almost contrary. To the philosopher who is thinking out a pantheistic system, or to the ascetic who is seeking after identity of consciousness with the One, the Hindu Avatars are only a part of the delusion, the Maya, in which men are steeped. To a pantheist, holding that his own consciousness of individuality is delusion, born of spiritual darkness and ignorance, the conception of an avatar or concrete presentation of deity as an individual is only still grosser delusion. "The name of God and the conventions of piety are as unreal as anything else in Maya," writes a modern British apostle of Hinduism, while advocating the realisation of Maya as our salvation.[88] It does not seem to me justifiable to say that through Pantheism the Indian mind can approach the thought of Christ the Son of Man and the Son of God. But pantheism, with its allied doctrine of transmigration, may encourage the thought that our Lord was a great jogi or religious devotee, the last climax of many upward transmigrations, and that Christ had attained to the goal of illumination of the jogi, namely, identity of consciousness with deity, when he felt "I and the Father are one." That statement about Our Lord is sometimes made in India.

---
The avatars of popular theology.
---

It is not through the pantheism of the brahmanically learned and of religious devotees that the Indian mind has come within Christ's sphere of influence, but rather through the beliefs of the multitude and the new education of the middle class. And how, we ask, has Christ been introduced to India by association with the popular beliefs—how, rather, has the attempt been made to do so? The theology of the people begins, as has been already stated, with the Hindu Triad, the three great personal deities, namely, Brahmā, Vishnu, and Siva,—Creator, Preserver, and Destroyer respectively. From these and other deities, but particularly from Vishnu, the Preserver, there descended to earth at various times and in various forms, human and animal, certain avatars.[89] Best known of these avatars of Vishnu, the Preserver, are Ram, the hero of the great epic called after him, the Rāmāyan; and secondly, Krishna, one of the chief figures of the other great Indian epic, the Mahābhārat; and thirdly, Buddha, the great religious teacher of the sixth century B.C. Ram and Krishna have become deities of the multitude over the greater part of India. Buddha, latest in time of these three avatars, and unknown as an avatar to the multitude, has not yet been lost to history. Such is the genealogy of certain of the Hindu gods and their avatars, and the object of setting it forth is to enable us to see how Jesus Christ has presented Himself or been presented to the Hindu people.

--------------------------------------------------------------------
Parallels in Christian and Hindu theology.
--------------------------------------------------------------------

When Christian doctrine was presented to India in modern times, the Christian Trinity and the Hindu Triad at once suggested a correspondence, which seemed to be confirmed by the coincidence of a Creator and Preserver in the Triad with the Creator and the Son, Our Saviour, in the Trinity. The historical Christ and the avatars of Vishnu would thus present themselves as at least striking theological and religious parallels. "On the one hand, learned brahmans have been found quite willing to regard Christ himself as an incarnation of Vishnu for the benefit of the Western world."[90] On the other, Christian missionaries in India have often preached Christ as the one true avatar.[91] The idea and the word *avatar* are always recurring in the hymns sung in Christian churches in India. Missionaries have also sought to graft the doctrine of Christ's atonement upon Hinduism, through one of the avatars. A common name of Vishnu, the second member of the Triad, as also of Krishna, his avatar, is *Hari*. Accepting the common etymology of *Hari* as meaning *the taker away*, Christian preachers have found an idea analogous to that of Christ, the Redeemer of men. Then the similarity of the names, *Christ* and *Krishna*, chief avatar of Vishnu, could not escape notice, especially since Krishna, Christ-like, is the object of the enthusiastic devotion of the Hindu multitude. In familiar speech, Krishna's name is still further approximated to that of Christ, being frequently pronounced *Krishta* or *Kishta*. In the middle of the nineteenth century the common opinion was that there was some historical connection between Krishna and Christ, and the idea lingers in the minds of both Hindus and Christians. One is surprised to find it in a recent European writer, formerly a member of the Indian Civil

Service. "Surely there is something more," he says, "than an analogy between Christianity and Krishna worship."[92]

Much has been made by the late Dr. K.M. Banerjea, the most learned member of the Indian Christian Church of the nineteenth century, and something also by the late Sir M. Monier Williams, of a passage in the Rigveda (x. 90), which seems to point to Christ. The passage speaks of Purusha (the universal spirit), who is also "Lord of Immortality," and was "born in the beginning," as having been "sacrificed by the Gods, Sadyas and Rishis," and as becoming thereafter the origin of the various castes and of certain gods and animals. A similar passage in a later book, the *Tāndya Brāhmanas*, declares that "the Lord of creatures, Prajapati, offered himself a sacrifice for the devas" (emancipated mortals or gods). Of the parallelism between the self-sacrificing Prajapati, Lord of creatures, and the Second Person in the Christian Trinity, propitiator and agent in creation, we may hear Dr. Banerjea himself: "The self-sacrificing Prajapati [Lord of creatures] variously described as Purusha, begotten in the beginning, as Viswakarma, the creator of all, is, in the meaning of his name and in his offices, identical with Jesus.... Jesus of Nazareth is the only person who has ever appeared in the world claiming the character and position of Prajapati, at the same time both mortal and immortal."[93]

---

These parallels ineffective.

---

Christ Himself attractive.

---

But it must be confessed that these parallels, real or supposed, between Christianity and Hinduism have not brought Christ home to the heart of India. In themselves, they only bring Christianity as near to Hinduism as they bring Hinduism to Christianity. Uneducated Hindus feel that the two religions are balanced when they have Krishna and Christians have Christ. Educated Hindus, as we shall see, are employing some of these very parallels to buttress Hinduism. Far be it from me, however, to depreciate the labours of scholars and earlier missionaries who have thus established links between Hindus and Christians, and have thus at least brought Christ into the Hindu's presence. To Indian Christians also such reasoning has often been a strength, furnishing as it were a new justification of their baptism into Christianity; for looking back they can perceive the finger of Hinduism itself pointing the way. But had no other influence been exerted on the Indian mind, one could not say what I now say, that Christ Himself is the feature of Christianity that has most powerfully moved men in India. The person of Christ Himself has been the great Christian dynamic. I am now speaking of educated India, the India that is not dependent solely upon the preacher for its religious ideas and feeling.

---

Christianity identified with Britain and therefore unpopular.

---

The anti-foreigner instinct.

---

The grand new political idea in India is the idea of nationality, and one of its corollaries is the championing of things Indian and depreciation of things British. The strong anti-British bias among the educated is one of the noteworthy and regrettable changes in the Indian mind within the last half-century. It is not surprising then that all over India the influence of Christ and of Christianity is lessened from the identification of Christianity with the British. For a native of India to accept the British religion is to run counter to the prevailing anti-British and pro-Indian feeling; it is unpatriotic to become a convert to Christianity. "Need we go out of India in quest of the true knowledge of God?" wrote a distinguished Indian littérateur a few years ago.[94] All that feeling is of course in addition to the instinctive hostility to things foreign that has been nowhere stronger than in self-contained India—self-contained between the Himalayas and the seas. The exclusiveness of caste is based upon that feeling. The statement of the late Rev. M.N. Bose, B.A., B.L., a native of Eastern Bengal, regarding his youth [1860?] is: "I had a deep-rooted prejudice against Christianity from my boyhood.... At this time I hated Christianity and Christians, though I knew not why I did so."[95] We find the instinctive hostility more bluntly expressed in China in the cry that drops spontaneously from the opening lips of many Chinamen, as their greeting, when they unexpectedly behold a European. The involuntary ejaculation is: "Strike the foreign devil."

---

Christ reverenced; Christians disliked.

---

In the first part of the nineteenth century, along with the great development of modern missions, and of modern education, we may say that Christ came again to India. The national and anti-British feeling had not then arisen to interpose in His path, but, coming as an alien, His name evoked great hostility. The popular mood was *Christianos ad leones,* as many incidents and witnesses testify. Now, in spite of the old anti-foreign hostility and the new currents of feeling, a remarkable attitude to Christianity—far short of conversion, no doubt—is almost everywhere manifest. There is a profound homage to its Founder, coupled with that strong resentment towards His Indian disciples. Christ Himself is acknowledged; His church is still foreign and British. Resentfully ruled by a Christian nation, but subdued by Christ Himself, is the state of educated India to-day. In spite of His alien birth and in spite of anti-British bias, Christ has passed within the pale of Indian recognition. Indian eyes, focused at last, are fastened upon Him, and men wonder at His gracious words. Again I direct attention to a significant event in Indian history—the incoming of an influence that will not stale, as mere ideas may. "Is there a single soul in this audience," said the Brahmo leader, the late Keshub Chunder Sen,[96] to the educated Indians of Calcutta, mostly Hindus, "who would scruple to ascribe extraordinary greatness and supernatural moral heroism to Jesus Christ and Him crucified?"

"That incarnation of the Divine Love, the lowly Son of man," writes another, even while he is rejoicing over the revival of Hinduism.[97]

# CHAPTER XVI

## JESUS CHRIST THE LODESTONE

"And I, if I be lifted up from the earth, will draw all men unto myself."

—ST. JOHN'S GOSPEL, xii. 32.

---

Instances of Indian homage to Christ, and dislike of His Church.

---

Bengal.

---

Bombay.

---

Madras.

---

Interesting phases of that divided mind—homage to Christ, resentment towards His disciples—may be found on opposite sides of the great continent of India. In Bengal, a not-infrequent standpoint of Brāhmas in reference to Christ is that *they* are the true exponents of Christ's spirit and His teaching. Western Christian teachers, they say, are hidebound by tradition; and the ready-made rigidity of the creeds of the Churches is no doubt a factor in the state of mind we are describing. Looking back as far as to 1820, we see in *The Precepts of Jesus*, published by the founder of the Brāhma Samāj, that standpoint of homage to Christ and dissent from accepted views regarding Him. Illustrative of that Brāhma standpoint, we have also the more recent book, *The Oriental Christ*, by the late Mr. P.C. Mozumdar, the successor of Keshub Chunder Sen. But the attitude is by no means limited to Brahmas. "Without Christian dogmas, cannot a man equally love and revere Christ?" was a representative question put by a senior Hindu student in Bengal to his missionary professor. In South India, Mahomedans sometimes actually describe themselves as better Christians than ourselves, holding as they do such faith in Jesus and His mother Mary and His Gospel. The case of Mahomedans is not, of course, on all fours with that of Hindus, since Mahomedans reckon Christ as one of the four prophets along with their own Mahomed. In Bombay province, on the other side of India from Bengal, we find Mr. Malabari, the famous Parsee, pupil of a Mission School, doubting if it is possible for the Englishman to be a Christian in the sense of *Christ's Christianity*, the implication being that an Indian may. What element of truth is there in the idea, we may well ask? From Indian Christians, be it said, we may indeed look for a fervency of loyalty to Christ that does not enter into our calculating moderate souls; and from India, equally, we may look for that mystically profound commentary on St. John's Gospel which Bishop Westcott declared he looked for from Japan. But to return. About Mr. Malabar! himself, his biographer writes: "If he could not accept the dogmas of Christianity, he had imbibed its true spirit," meaning the spirit of Christ Himself. "The cult of the Asiatic life" is the latest definition of Christianity given by a recent apologist of Hinduism, one of a small company of Europeans in India officering the Hindu revival. Crossing India again and going south, we find the late Dr. John Murdoch, of Madras, an eminent observer, adding his testimony regarding the homage paid to the Founder of Christianity. "The most hopeful sign," he writes, "is the increasing reverence for our Lord, although His divinity is not yet acknowledged."[98] And of new India generally, again, we may quote Mr. Bose, the Indian historian. "The Christianity [of North-western Europe] is no more like Christianity as preached by Christ than the Buddhism of the Thibetans is like Buddhism as preached by Gautama." Take finally the following sentences from a recent number of a moderate neo-Hindu organ, the *Hindustan Review (vol.* viii. 514): "Christ, the great exemplar of practical morality ...; the more one enters into the true spirit of Christ, the more will he reject Christianity as it prevails in the world to-day. The Indians have been gainers not losers by rejecting Christianity for the sake of Christ."[99]

---

Desire to discover Christian ideas in Hindu Scriptures.

---

Christ and Krishna set alongside.

---

Another phase of that same divided mind, acknowledging Christ and resenting Indian discipleship, may be perceived in the willingness to discover Christian ideas in Hindu Scriptures, and Christ-like features in Hindu deities and religious heroes. To express it from the Indian standpoint,—they see Christ and Christianity bringing back much of their own "refined and modernised." In a sense, as a Bengali Christian gentleman put it, Christ and Christianity have become the accepted standards in religion.[100] Again we quote from the same page of the *Hindustan Review.* "A revival of Hinduism has taken place.... It [Christianity] has given us Christ, and given us noble moral and spiritual lessons, which we have discovered anew in our own Scriptures, and thereby satisfied our self-love and made our very own." We have mentioned how missionaries used to find the doctrine of the atonement in the name of the Indian God Hari; the argument has now in turn been annexed by Hindus, and employed as an argument in their favour. Within the last twenty years, there has been a great revival of the honouring of Krishna among the educated classes in Bengal and the United Provinces. Krishna has set up distinctly as the Indian Christ, or as the Indian figure to be set up over against Christ. A Krishna story has been disentangled from the gross mythology, and he has become a paragon of virtue,—the work of a distinguished Bengali novelist. I mean no sarcasm. From the sermon of a Hindu preacher in a garden in Calcutta in 1898, I quote: "The same God came into the world as the Krishna of India and the Krishna of Jerusalem." These are his words. From the catalogue of the Neo-Krishnaite literature in Bengal, given by Mr. J.N. Farquhar of the Y.M.C.A., Calcutta, it appears that since 1884 thirteen Lives of Krishna or works on Krishna have appeared in Bengal. Many essays have appeared comparing Krishna with Christ. There have been likewise many editions of the Bhagabat Gita, or Divine Song, the episode in the Mahabharat, in which Krishna figures as religious teacher. It may be called the New Testament of the Neo-Krishnaite. Perhaps the most striking of these Neo-Krishnaite publications is *The Imitation of Sri-Krishna*, a daily-text book containing extracts from the Bhagabat Gita and the Bhagabat Puran. The title is, of course, a manifest echo of "The Imitation of Christ," which is a favourite with religious-minded Hindus. The *Imitation of Buddha*, likewise we may observe, has been published. About "The Imitation of Christ" itself, we quote from a Hindu's advertisement appended to the life of a new Hindu saint, Ramkrishna Paramhansa. "The reader of 'The Imitation of Christ,'" it says, "will find echoed in it hundreds of sayings of our Lord Sri-Krishna in the Bhagabat Gita like the following: 'Give up all religious work and come to me as thy sole refuge, and I will deliver thee from all manner of sin.'" The notice goes on: "The book has found its way into the pockets of many orthodox Hindus."

---

Christ and Chaitanya of Bengal.

---

From Krishna we turn to Chaitanya, surname Gauranga, the fair, a religious teacher of Bengal in the fifteenth century, who is also being set up as the Christ of Bengal, in that he preached the equality of men before God and ecstatic devotion to the god Krishna. A Christ-like man, indeed, in many ways, Chaitanya was, and the increased acquaintance of educated Bengal with Jesus Christ naturally brought Chaitanya to the front. The new cult of Chaitanya and his enthronement over against Jesus Christ are manifest in the titles of two recent publications in Bengal, the first entitled, *Lord Gauranga, or Salvation for all*, and the other, *Chaitanya's Message of Love*. Chaitanya and his two chief followers, it should be said, were called the great *lords* (prabhus) of the sect, but the title "Lord Gauranga" is quite new, an echo of the title of Jesus Christ. With regard to the new power of Christ's personality, it should be noted that the author of *Lord Gauranga* strongly deprecates the idea that his desire is to demolish Christianity, or other than to extend the kingdom of Jesus Christ. He declares that Jesus Christ is as much a prophet as any avatar of the Hindus, and that Hindus can and ought to accept him as they do Krishna or Chaitanya. This is in accord with the spirit of Hinduism—namely, the fluidity of doctrine, and the free choice of guru or religious teacher, as set forth in a previous chapter—although it is still an advanced position for a Hindu to take up publicly.

---

Eccentric manifestations of the power of Christ's personality.

---

Could we observe the course of evolution down which a species of animals or plants has come from some remote ancestry to their present form, with what interest would we note the specific characteristics gathering strength, as from generation to generation they prove their "fitness to survive"! The whole onward career of the evolving species would seem to have been aimed at the latest form in which we find it. Yet quite as wonderful phenomena as the species that has survived are the many variations of the species that have presented themselves, but have not proved fit to survive. One species only survives for hundreds of would-be collaterals that are extinct. The religious evolution that we have been observing is the growing power of Christ's personality in New India; and now, as further testimony to its power, a number of collateral movements, similarly inspired yet eccentric and hardly likely to endure, attract our attention. In these eccentric movements the power of Christ's personality is manifest, and yet it appears amid circumstances so peculiar that the phenomena in themselves are grotesque.

---

The Punjab—two have set themselves up as Christ come again.

---

Hakim Singh.

---

Mirzā Gholām Ahmad.

---

Three of these strange movements let us look at as new evidence of the power of Christ's personality in India. All three occur in still another province than those named, the Punjab, a province *sui generis* in many ways. Within a generation past, at least two men have arisen, either claiming to be Christ Himself come again, or a Messiah superior to Him. A third received a vision of "Jesus God," and proclaimed Him, wherever he went, as an object of worship. Of the first of the three leaders, Sir Alfred Lyall tells us, one Hakim Singh, "who listened to missionaries until he not only accepted the whole Christian dogma, but conceived himself to be the second embodiment [of Christ], and proclaimed himself as such and summoned the missionaries to acknowledge him." It sounds much like blasphemy, or mere lunacy; but in India one learns not to be shocked at what in Europe would be rankest blasphemy; the intention must decide the innocence or the offence. Hakim Singh "professed to work miracles, preached pure morality, but also venerated the cow,"—strange chequer of Hindu and Christian ideas.[101] The second case is the better known one of Mirzā Gholām Ahmad, of Qādiān, who sets up a claim to be "the Similitude of the Messiah" and "the Messiah of the Twentieth Century." As his name shows, he is a Mahomedan, but the assumption of the name "Messiah" also shows that it is in Christ's place he declares himself to stand. At the same time, his appeal is to his fellow-Mahomedans; for he explains that as Jesus was the Messiah of Moses, he himself is the Messiah of Mahomed. His superiority to Christ, he expressly declares. "I shall be guilty of concealing the truth," he says in his English monthly, the *Review of Religions*, of May 1902, "if I do not assert that the prophecies which God Almighty has granted me are of a far better quality in clearness, force, and truth than the ambiguous predictions of Jesus.... But notwithstanding all this superiority, I cannot assert Divinity or Sonship of God." He claims "to have been sent by God to reform the true religion of God, now corrupted by Jews, Christians, and Mahomedans." Doubly blasphemous as his claims sound in the ears of orthodox Mahomedans, who reckon both Christ and Mahomed as prophets, his sect is now estimated to number at least 10,000, including many educated Mahomedans. Whatever its fate—a mere comet or a new planet in the Indian sky—it indicates the religious stirring of educated India in another province, and the prominence of Christ's personality therein. Mirzā Gholām Ahmad himself recommends the reading of the Gospels. As to Christ's death, Mirzā Gholām Ahmad has a theory of his own. The Koran declares, according to Mahomedan expositors, that it was not Christ who suffered on the cross, but another in His likeness. Mirzā Gholām Ahmad teaches that Jesus was crucified but did not die, that He was restored to life by His disciples and sent out of the country, whence He travelled East until He reached Thibet, eventually arriving at Cashmere, where He died, His tomb being located in the city of Srinagar.[102]

According to the latest report of this reincarnation, he now claims to be at once Krishna come again for Hindus, Mahomed for Mahomedans, and Christ for Christians.

┌─────────────────────────────────────────────────────────────────────┐
⋮  Chet Ram claimed to be an apostle.                                   ⋮
└─────────────────────────────────────────────────────────────────────┘

The third movement is that of the Chet Ramis, or sect of Chet Ram, whose strange history may be found in *East and West* for July 1905. Chet Ram was an illiterate Hindu, a water-carrier and then a steward in the Indian army that took part in the war with China in 1859-1860. Returning to his native district not far from Lahore, Chet Ram, the Hindu, came under the spell of a Mahomedan ascetic Mahbub Shāh, left all and followed him as his "familiar" disciple. How this relationship between Hindu and Mahomedanism is quite possible in India, we have already explained on pages 163-4; Mahbub Shāh's strange combination of religious asceticism with the consumption of opium and wine, it takes some years' residence in India to understand. Then Mahbub Shāh died, and the disciple succeeded the master. According to one account, Chet Ram made his bed on the grave in which his master lay; according to another, for three years his sleeping place was the vault within which his master was buried. It was at this time that he had the vision of "Jesus God," already referred to, between the years 1860 and 1865. Like Caedmon, he has described his vision in verse—

"Upon the grave of Master Mahbub Shah
Slept Sain Chet Earn.

A man came in a glorious form,
Showing a face of mercy.

Sweet was his speech and simple his face,
Appearing entirely as the image of God.

He called aloud, 'Who sleeps there?
Awake, if thou art sleeping.
Thou art distinctly fortunate,
Thou art needed in the Master's presence.'

'Build a church on this very spot,
Place the Bible therein.'

Then said that luminous form,
Jesus, the image of Mary:

'I shall do justice in earth and heaven,
And reveal the hidden mysteries.'

Astonished there alone I stood,
As if a parrot had flown out of my hands.

Then my soul realised
That Jesus came to give salvation.

I realised that it was Jesus God
Who appeared in a bodily form."[103]

---

The Followers of Chet Ram.

---

Their indefinite composite theology.

---

Whence came the Christian seed of Chet Ram's vision? His master Mahbub Shah was a Mahomedan, and Jesus Christ is reckoned one of the Mahomedan prophets. But it is the Christ of Christianity, not of Mahomedanism, that Chet Ram saw in his vision of the glorious form showing the face of mercy, at once the dispenser of justice, the revealer of mysteries, and the giver of salvation. Whatever the source of the vision, Chet Ram saw and believed and began to hold up Jesus Christ before other men's eyes, and Chet Ram himself thus became the guru or religious teacher of what may be called an indigenous Christian Church. A moderate estimate reckons the Chet Ramis at about five thousand souls, the religious force of the sect being represented by the Chet Rami ascetics, who go about making their gospel known and living on alms. Chet Ram himself died in 1894, and at the headquarters of the sect at Buchhoke, near Lahore, his ashes and the bones of his master Mahbub Shah are kept in two coffins, which the faithful visit, particularly on certain Chet Rami holy-days, on which fairs are held. In keeping with the command of the vision, several copies of the New Testament and one complete Bible were also on view when the writer of the article in *East and West* visited the sanctuary in 1903. The *Census Report* for 1901 sums the Chet Ramis up by saying that "the sect professes a worship of Christ," and that is our present point of view. But we cannot leave them without noticing also how Indian they are in their unwillingness to define their thought, and in their readiness to enthrone a holy man and his relics. Undefined thought we see expressed in symbol. There are *four* doors to the sanctuary at Buchhoke,—the fakiri [Chet Rami ascetics'] door, the Hindu, Christian, and Mahomedan doors—expressing the openness of the Chet Rami sanctuary to all sects. Their theology is a corresponding conglomeration. It includes a Christian trinity of Jesus Son of Mary [the Mahomedan designation of Christ], the Holy Spirit, and God; and a Hindu triad of the world's three potencies, namely, Allah, Parameswar, and Khuda, a jumble of Hindu and Mahomedan names, but representing the Hindu triad of the Creator, Preserver, and Destroyer.

> Parallel between the nineteenth century in India and the second, third, and fourth centuries in the History of the Church.

> The Theosophists and the Neo-Platonists.

> The Neo-Platonists and New India's homage to Christ.

> The Neo-Platonists and the Hindu Revivalists.

In respect of the phenomenon of the homage shown to Christ over against the hostility shown to His Church, the second, third, and fourth centuries in the history of the Church present a striking parallel to the nineteenth century in India. Steadily in these centuries Christianity was progressing in spite of contempt for its adherents, philosophic repudiation of the doctrines of the *superstitio prava*, and official persecution unknown in British India at least. Then also, as always, Christ stood out far above His followers, lifted up and drawing all men's eyes. Such in India also, in the nineteenth century, has been the course of Christianity; parts of the record of these centuries read like the record of the religious movements in India in these latter days. Describing the Neo-Platonists of these centuries, historians tell us that at the end of the second century A.D. Ammonius of Alexandria, founder of the sect, "undertook to bring all systems of philosophy and religion into harmony, by which all philosophers and men of all religions, Christianity included, might unite and hold fellowship." *There* are the four doors of the Chet Rami sanctuary. There also we have the Theosophical Society of India, professing in its constitution to be "the nucleus of a Universal Brotherhood of Humanity, representing and excluding no religious creed." Ammonius, founder of the Neo-Platonists, was a pantheist like the present leader of the Theosophical Society, Mrs. Besant, and like her too, curiously, had begun as a Christian.[104] We recall that of Indian Theosophy in general, in 1891, the late Sir Monier Williams declared that it seemed little more than another name for the "Vedanta [or

Pantheistic] philosophy." Exactly like the earlier theosophists also, Ammonius, the Neo-Platonist, held that the purified soul could perform physical wonders, by the power of Theurgy. In its constitution the Theosophical Society professed "to investigate the hidden mysteries of nature and the psychical powers latent in man." Many can remember how, in the eighties, Madame Blavatsky took advantage of our curiosity regarding such with air-borne letters from Mahatmas in Thibet. Again Ammonius, we read, "turned the whole history of the pagan gods into allegory." There we have the Neo-Krishnaites of to-day. "He acknowledged that Christ was an extraordinary man, the friend of God, and an admirable Theurgus." There we have the stand point of the educated Indians who have come under Christ's spell. For two centuries the successors of Ammonius followed in these lines. "Individual Neo-Platonists," Harnack tells us, "employed Christian sayings as oracles, and testified very highly of Christ. Porphyry of Syria, chief of the Neo-Platonists of the third century, wrote a work "against Christians"; but again, according to Harnack, the work is not directed against Christ, or what Porphyry regarded as the teaching of Christ. It was directed against the Christians of his day and against the sacred books, which according to Porphyry were written by impostors and ignorant people. There we have the double mind of educated India,— homage to Christ, opposition to His Church. There also we have the standpoint of Sahib Mirza Gholam Ahmad of Qadian. Some, we read, being taught by the Neo-Platonists that there was little difference between the ancient religion, rightly explained and restored to its purity, and the religion which Christ really taught, not that corrupted form of it which His disciples professed, concluded it best for them to remain among those who worshipped the gods. There is the present Indian willingness to discover Christian and modern ideas in the Hindu Scriptures, especially in the original Vedas that the new Ārya sect declare to be "the Scripture of true knowledge." The practical outcome of the Neo-Platonic movement was an attempt to revive the old Græco-Roman religion,—Julian the apostate emperor had many with him. There we have the revival of the worship of Krishna in India, and the apologies for idolatry and caste. The most recent stage of the Theosophical Society in India reveals *it* as virtually a Hindu revival society. Finally, we read, the old philosopher Pythagoras, Apollonius of Tyana, and others were represented on the stage dressed in imitation of Christ Himself, and the Emperor Alexander Severus [A.D. 222-235] placed the figure of Christ in his lararium alongside of those of Abraham, Orpheus, and Apollonius. There we have the modern Indians who fully recognise Christ alongside of their own avatars. The whole parallel is complete.[105] In spite of the feebleness and, it may be, unworthiness of His Church, through the force of Christ's personality, the Roman history of the second, third, and fourth centuries has been repeating itself in India in the nineteenth and twentieth, and unless the force of Christ's personality be spent, the parallels will proceed.

From new reasonings about God, her new monotheism, New India has been brought a stage farther to actual history. From theologies she has come to the first three Gospels. New India has been introduced to Christ as He actually lived on earth before men's eyes; and to India, intensely interested in religious teachers, the personality of the Christ of the Gospels, of the first three Gospels in particular, appeals strongly. To the pessimistic mood of India He appeals as one whose companionship makes this life more worth living; for Christ was not a jogi in the Indian sense of a renouncer of the world. His call to fraternal service has taken firm hold of the best Indians of to-day. Of the future we know not, but we feel that the narrative of the first three Gospels naturally precedes the deeper insight of the fourth.

# CHAPTER XVII

## INDIAN PESSIMISM—ITS BEARING ON BELIEF IN THE HERE AND HEREAFTER

"How many births are past, I cannot tell:
How many yet to come, no man can say:
But this alone I know, and know full well,
That pain and grief embitter all the way."

(*South-Indian Folk-song*, quoted in *Lux Christi*, by Caroline
Atwater Mason.)

"When desire is gone, and the cords of the heart are broken,
then the soul is delivered from the world and is at rest in
God."

---

Indian pessimism.

---

Two commonplaces about India are that pessimism is her natural
temperament, and that a natural outcome of her pessimism is the Indian
doctrine of the transmigration of souls. The second statement will require
explanation; but as regards the former, there is no denying the strain of
melancholy, the note of hopelessness, that pervades these words we have
quoted, or that they are characteristic of India. In them life seems a burden;
to be born into it, a punishment; and of the transmigrations of our souls
from life to life, seemingly, we should gladly see the end. All the same, as
new India is proving, pessimism is not the inherent temperament of India,
and the hope of the end of the transmigration, and of the lives of the soul,
no more natural in India than in any other land.

---

Due to nature?

---

Pessimism is natural in India, say such writers as we have in mind, because
of the spirit-subduing aspects of nature and life amid which Indians live
their lives. Life is of little value to the possessor, they say, where nature

makes it a burden, and where its transitoriness is constantly being thrust upon us. And that is so in India. Great rivers keep repeating their contemptuous motto that "men may come and men may go," and by their floods sometimes devastate whole districts. Sailing up the Brahmaputra at one place in Assam, the writer saw a not uncommon occurrence, the great river actually eating off the soft bank in huge slices, five or six feet in breadth at a time. Something higher up, it might have been the grounding of a floating tree, had turned the current towards the bank, and at five-minute intervals, it seemed, these huge slices were falling in. Not fifty yards back from the bank stood a cottage, whose garden was already part gone; a banana tree standing upon one of these slices fell in and was swept down before our eyes. Within an hour the cottage itself would meet the same fate, and the people were already rushing in and out. Or pass to another aspect of nature. For a season every year the unveiled Indian sun in a sky of polished steel glares with cruel pitiless eye. The light is fierce. Then, arbitrarily, as it seems, the rains may be withheld, and the hard-baked, heat-cracked soil never softens to admit the ploughshare, and hundreds of thousands of the cultivators and field hands are overtaken by famine. At one time during the famine of 1899-1900, it will be remembered that six million people were receiving relief. Or, equally arbitrarily, betokening some unknown displeasure of the gods, plague may take hold of a district and literally take its tithe of the population. At any moment, life is liable to be terminated with appalling suddenness by cholera or the bite of a venomous serpent.

With French imagination and grace, in his *Introduction to General History*, Michelet describes the tyranny of nature—"Natura maligna"—in India. "Man is utterly overpowered by nature there—like a feeble child upon a mother's breast, alternately spoiled and beaten, and intoxicated rather than nourished by a milk too strong and stimulating for it."[106] One cannot help contrasting the supplicating Indian villagers—of whom a University matriculation candidate told in his essay, how, when the rains were withheld, they carried out the village goddess from her temple and bathed the idol in the temple tank—with the English fisher-woman of whom Tennyson tells us, who shook her fist at the cruel sea that had robbed her of two sons. As she looked at it one day with its lines of white breakers, she shook her fist at it and told it her mind—"How I hates you, with your cruel teeth."

Can this Indian aspect of nature, one wonders, be the true explanation of the fierceness of her goddesses as contrasted with her gods, and the offering of bloody sacrifices to goddesses only? Mother Nature is malignant, not benign.

The value of life and the little worth of life in India may be gauged in another way. In the language of the political economist, the value of human life in any country may be estimated by the average wage, which determines the standard of comfort and how far a man is restricted to the bare necessities of bodily life. Again, judged by that standard, life is probably in no civilised country at a lower estimate than in India, where the labourer spends over 90 per. cent of his income upon the bare necessities for the sustenance of the bodies of his household.

Indian pessimism only a mood.

Humanlife is rising in value

Pessimism is declining

All that is true, and yet the conclusion is only partly true. In spite of all such reasoning, and acknowledging that the physical characteristics of India have largely made her what she is, politically, socially, and even religiously, I venture to think that the pessimism of India is exaggerated. Not a pessimistic temperament, but a mood, a mood of helpless submissiveness, a bowing to the powers that be in nature and in the world, seems to me the truer description of the prevailing "pessimism." At least, if it be the case, as I have tried to show, that during the past century in India, human life has been rising in value, the pessimistic mood must be declining. Let us observe some facts again. In a Government or Mission Hospital, *there* is a European doctor taking part in the offensive work of the dressing of a coolie's sores,—we assume that the doctor's touch is the touch of a true Christian gentleman. To the despised sufferer, life is gaining a new sweetness, and to the high-caste student looking on and ready to imitate his teacher, life is attaining a new dignity. That human life has been rising in value is patent. The wage of the labourer has been steadily rising—in one or two places the workers are become masters of the situation; the rights of woman are being recognised, if only slowly; the middle classes are eager for education and advancement; the individual has been gaining in independence as the tyranny of caste and custom has declined; the sense of personal security and of citizenship and of nationality has come into being. Whatever the merits of the great agitation in 1905 against the partition of the Province of Bengal, and inconceivable as taking place a century ago, it is manifestly the doing of men keenly interested in the conditions under which they live. It is a contradiction of the theory of an inherent Indian pessimism. Self-respect and a sense of the dignity and duties of manhood are surely increasing, and making our earth a place of hope and making life worth living, instead of a burden to be borne. "The Hindus," says Sir Alfred Lyall, "have been rescued by the English out of a chronic state of anarchy, insecurity, lawlessness, and precarious exposure to the caprice of despots."[107]

---

Asceticism is declining.

---

Best proof probably that pessimism is declining is the fact that asceticism is declining. The times are no longer those in which the life of a brahman is supposed to culminate in the Sannyasi or ascetic "who has laid down everything," who, in the words of the Bhagabat Gita, "does not hate and does not love anything."[108] The pro-Hindu writer often quoted also acknowledges the new pleasure in life and the religious corollary of it when she says that the recent rise in the standard of comfort in India is opposed to the idea of asceticism. Desire, indeed, is not gone, and the cords of the heart are not breaking. Says the old brahman, in the guise of whom Sir Alfred Lyall speaks: "I own that you [Britons] are doing a great deal to soften and enliven material existence in this melancholy, sunburnt country of ours, and certainly you are so far successful that you are bringing the ascetic idea into discouragement and, with the younger folk, into contempt."[109] Welcome to the new joy of living, all honour to the old ascetics, and may a still nobler self-sacrifice take their place!

---

Pessimism, asceticism, transmigration are allied ideas.

---

For Western minds it is difficult to realise the close connection between the doctrine of transmigration and the mood of India, rightly or wrongly termed pessimism. *Our* instinctive feeling is that life is sweet; while there is life there is hope, *we* say; "*healthy* optimism" is the expression of Professor James in his *Varieties of Religious Experience*; it is "*more life* and fuller that we want." In keeping with this Western and human instinct, the Christian idea of the Hereafter is a fuller life than the life Here, a perfect eternal life. To the pessimist, on the contrary [and Hindu philosophy is pessimistic, whatever be the new mood of India], the question is, "Why was I born?" The Indian doctrine of transmigration comes with answer—"Life is a punishment: it is the bitter consequence of our past that we are working out; we must *submit* to be born into the world again and again, until we are cleared." "Yes, until your minds are cleared," the Indian pantheist adds, "life *itself* is a delusion, if you only knew it; life itself, your consciousness of individuality or separateness, is a delusion." But the pantheist's thought is here beside our present point.

---

Transmigration the antithesis of eternal life.

---

To the pessimistic Indian accepting the Indian view of transmigration, it is therefore no gospel to preach the continuation of life, either here or hereafter. "To be born again" sounds like a penance to be endured. *Mukti*, commonly rendered *salvation*, is not regeneration Here and eternal life Hereafter; it is *deliverance* from further lives altogether. If, however, we accept the statement that the value of human life in India is rising, that life is becoming worth living, and that the pessimistic mood is no ingrained fundamental trait, we are prepared to believe that the hopeful Christian conception of the Here and the Hereafter is finding acceptance. Rightly understood, the Christian conception is at bottom the antithesis of pessimism and its corollary, transmigration. To deny the one is almost to assert the other. The decay of the one is the growth of the other. For the Christian conception of the Here and the Hereafter—what is it? Life, eternal, in and through the Spirit of Jesus Christ, the Son of God. "God gave unto us eternal life, and the life is in His Son. He that hath the Son hath the life."[110] Says Harnack in his volume *What is Christianity?* "The Christian religion means one thing, and one thing only—eternal life in the midst of time by the strength and under the eyes of God." Not that the new idea in India is to be wholly ascribed to Christian influence. A marked change in Christian thought itself during the nineteenth century has been the higher value of this present life. Christianity has become a vitalising gospel for the life Here even more than for the Hereafter. But assuming the truth of what we have sought to show, namely, that within the past century the winning personality of Christ has come to New India, a new incentive to noble life and service, we have at least a further reason for believing that pessimism and transmigration are fading out of Indian minds. The new Advent, as that at Bethlehem, is a turning-point of time; the gloomy winter of pessimism is turning to a hopeful spring.

# CHAPTER XVIII

## INDIAN TRANSMIGRATION AND THE CHRISTIAN HERE AND HEREAFTER

"The dew is on the lotus. Rise, good sun!
And lift my leaf and mix me with the wave.
The sunrise comes!
The dewdrop slips into the shining sea.

If any teach Nirvana is to cease,
Say unto such they lie.
If any teach Nirvana is to live,
Say unto such they err."

(Buddha's teaching in Arnold's *Light of Asia*.)

> Over against Transmigration, Christian immortality is continuity of the individual's memory.

To appreciate the impact of the Christian idea of the Here and Hereafter upon the Hindu idea of Transmigration and Absorption, the two ideas must be more fully examined. Stated briefly, the Christian idea is that after this life on earth comes an Eternity, whose character has been determined by the life on earth. The crisis of death terminates our bodily activities and renders impossible any further action, either virtuous or sinful, and ushers the soul, its ledger closed, its earthy limitations cast off, into some more immediate presence of God. If in communion with God, through its faith in Jesus Christ, the soul is in a state of blessedness; if still alien from God, the soul is in a state of utter misery, for its spiritual perception and its recollection of itself are now clear. That, at all events, seems a fair statement of the belief of many Protestants, so far as their belief is definite at all. But over against transmigration, what are the essential and distinctive features of that Christian belief? Its essentially distinctive feature, both in the case of the blessed and of the miserable, is a *continuity* of the consciousness in the life that now is with that which is to come. The soul in bliss or misery is able to associate its existing state with its past. Even on earth, as the modern preacher tells us, heaven and hell are already begun.

Over against the Hindu idea of transmigration, accordingly, we define the Christian idea of immortality as the continuity of our consciousness, or the immortality of the individual consciousness.

Transmigration is essentially dissolution of the individual's memory.

Per contra, the distinguishing feature of the Hindu doctrine of transmigration or rebirth is the interruption of consciousness, the dissolution of memory, at the close of the present existence. In the next existence there is no memory of the present.

"The draught of Lethe" does "await
The slipping through from state to state."

The present life is a member of a series of lives; there are said to be 8,400,000 of them, each member of which is as unconscious of the preceding as you are of being I. As a seed develops into plant and flower and seed again, so the soul in each new member of the series develops a conscious life, lapses from consciousness, and hands on a germinal soul for a new beginning again. As the seed transmits the type, and also some variation from the type, so is the germinal soul transmitted through unconsciousness, ennobled or degraded by each conscious existence it has lived. At each stage the germinal soul represents the totality, the net outcome of its existences, as in each generation of a plant the seed may be said to do. So far, the doctrine of transmigration is a doctrine of the evolution of a soul, a declaration that in a sense we are all that we have been, that virtue and vice will have their reward, that in a sense "men may rise on stepping stones of their dead selves." It does not leave hard cases of heathen or of reprobates to the discernment and mercy of God; it offers them, instead, other chances in subsequent lives. A not unattractive doctrine it is, even although the attractive analogy of the evolution of a plant breaks down. For in the scientific doctrine of evolution, individuals have no immortality *at all*; it is only the species that lives and moves on. But in Hinduism, as in Christianity, we are thinking of the continuity of the *individual* souls.

The end of transmigration is absorption into Deity.

The saint Ramkrishna's obliviousness of self.

To proceed with the statement of the doctrine of transmigration. The climax of the transmigrations is Nirvana or extinction of the individual soul, according to the Buddhist, and union with or absorption into Deity, according to the Hindu.[111] Buddhism has gone from the land of its birth, as Christianity and even Judaism from Palestine, and I pass from the Buddhist doctrine. The Hindu climax, of absorption into Deity, is reached when by self-mastery personal desire is gone, and by profound contemplation upon Deity a pure-bred soul has lost the consciousness of separation from Deity. The distinction between *I* and the great *Thou* has vanished; the One is present in the mind not as an objective thought, but by a transformation of the consciousness itself. The words of Hindus themselves in the *Advanced Text-book of Hindu Religion* are: The human soul (the Jivatmic seed) "grows into self-conscious Deity." Listen also to the words of Swami Vivekananda, in the Parliament of Religions, Chicago, about his master, Ramkrishna Paramhansa's growing into self-conscious Deity: "Every now and then strange fits of God-consciousness came upon him.... He then spoke of himself as being able to do and know everything.... He would speak of himself as the same soul that had been born before as Rama, as Krishna, as Jesus, or as Buddha, born again as Ramkrishna.... He would say he was ... an incarnation of God Himself." Again Swami Vivekananda tells us: "From time to time Ramkrishna would entirely lose his own identity, so much so as to appropriate to himself the offerings brought for the goddess" (to the temple in which he officiated). "Sometimes forgetting to adorn the image, he would adorn *himself* with the flowers."[112] Transmigration is not necessarily bound up with the pantheistic view of the world, but in *Hinduism*, transmigration is only a ladder towards the realisation of the One.

> Contrasts—"Born again" and a spiritual aristocracy of long spiritual descent.

> Heaven and Hell not necessary ideas in Transmigration.

Radical differences from Christian thought emerge. In the Hindu conception, the acme is reached only by a spiritual aristocracy of long spiritual descent; for the common multitude there is no gospel of being born again in Christ, no guiding hand like that of Our Lord towards the Father's presence. The upward path, according to the Hindu idea, is the path of philosophical knowledge and of meditation, not the power of union with Jesus Christ to make us sons of God. Most striking difference perhaps of all—in the Hindu philosophical system there is no place for even the conceptions of heaven and hell except as temporary halting-places between two incarnations of the soul, which practical necessity requires. For the soul, this world is the plane of existence; union with omnipresent Deity is the climax of existence that the Hindu devotee seeks to attain; yet not in a Hereafter, but as he sits on the ground no longer conscious of his self. "The beatific vision of Hinduism," says a recent pro-Hindu writer, "is to be relegated to no distant future."[113] Heaven and Hell are mocked at as absurdities by the new sect of the Āryas in the United Provinces and the Punjab, who retain the doctrine of transmigration.[114]

---

Several heavens and hells in popular Hinduism.

---

Hindus are divided as to the existence of these temporary halting-places between the successive incarnations of the soul. The *Text-book of Hindu Religion*, already referred to, speaks unhesitatingly about their place in the Hindu system. The Āryas, on the other hand, hold that the instant a soul leaves its body it enters another body just born. The soul is never naked— to employ a common figure. Of course in popular Hinduism it is not surprising to find not merely the ideas of Heaven and Hell, but even that each chief Deity has his own heaven and that there are various hells. In the Tantras or ritual books of modern Hinduism, there is frequent mention of such heavens and hells, and when the idea of rebirths is also met with, the rebirths are regarded as stages towards the reward or punishment of the *individual conscious* souls. It is the popular idea of heaven that has given rise to the common euphemism for *to die*, namely, to become a deva or inhabitant of heaven.

---

Transmigration, associated with pessimism and pantheism, is likewise yielding.

---

We have observed the pessimistic mood of India yielding before the improved conditions of life, and the brahmanical pantheism before the thought of God the Father. Bound up as the idea of transmigration has been with the pessimism and pantheism of India, we are prepared to find that it too is yielding. Of that we now ask what evidence there is in the ordinary speech and writings of educated India, apart from controversy or professedly Hindu writings, in which the accepted Indian orthodoxy would probably appear.

---

Educated Hindus speak of the dead as if their former consciousness continued.

---

From the ordinary speeches and writings of educated Hindus regarding the dead, no one would infer that their doctrinal standpoint was other than that of the ordinary religious Briton, namely, that the dead friend has returned to God or has been called away by God, or the like. A native judge in Bengal, one of the most distinguished leaders of the Hindu Revival, writes as follows: The beatitude which the new Radha-Krishnaites aspire to "is not the Nirvana of the Vedantists, the quiescence of Rationalism. Nirvana and quiescence are merely negatives. The beatitude [of the new Radha-Krishnaites] is a positive something. They do not aspire to unification with the divine essence. They prefer hell with its torments to such unification."[115] A few years ago, at a public meeting in Calcutta, the acknowledged leader of Hinduism, speaking of a Hindu gentleman whose death we were lamenting, said: "God has taken him to himself"—certainly not a Hindu statement of the passing of a soul. Similarly, in 1882 we find one nobleman in Bengal writing to another regarding his mother's death: "It is my prayer to God that she may abide in eternal happiness in heaven."[116] Generations of Hindu students I have known to find pleasure in identifying themselves with Wordsworth's views of immortality:

"Trailing clouds of glory do we come
From God who is our home,"

and

"The faith that looks through death."

------------------------------------------------------------
Transmigration now no more than a conventional explanation of how misfortunes befell one.
------------------------------------------------------------

Somewhat dreamlike Wordsworth's views may be, but his belief is clearly not in transmigration. To the educated Hindu, who may not consciously have rejected the idea of transmigration, the doctrine is really now no more than a current and convenient explanation of any misfortune that has befallen a person. "Why has it befallen him? He must have earned it in some previous existence. It is in the debit balance of the transactions in his lives." Such are the vague ideas floating in the air. Upon any individual's acts or plans for the future, the idea of transmigration seems to have no bearing whatever beyond a numbing of the will.[117] For in theory, the Hindu's fate is just. In strict logic no doubt the same numbing effect might be alleged about the Christian doctrine of predestination. Even when misfortune has overtaken an educated Hindu, I think I am justified in saying that the more frequent thought with him is now in keeping with the new theistic belief; the misfortune is referred to the will of God. As already said, it is a commonplace of the unfortunate student who has failed, to ascribe his failure to God's will.

------------------------------------------------------------
Transmigration and Predestination more properly contrasted.
------------------------------------------------------------

There is room for the Christian thought of the Hereafter, because in reality, as theologians know, the doctrine of transmigration stands over against the Christian doctrine of predestination rather than over against the Christian doctrine of the Here and Hereafter. Transmigration is a doctrine of what has gone before the present life rather than of what will follow. Every educated Anglo-Indian whom I have consulted agrees that in a modern Hindu's mouth transmigration is only a theory of the incidence of actual suffering. Here is the doctrine of *karma* (works), that is of transmigration or merited rebirth, in the actual life of India— transmigration and the pessimistic helplessness of which I have spoken? In the last great famine of 1899-1900, in a village in South-western India, a missionary found a victim of famine lying on one side of the village street, and not far off, upon the other side, two or three men of the middle class. The missionary reproached them for their callousness. What might be answered for them is not here to the point; their answer for themselves was, "It is his *karma*." The missionary did what he could for the famine sufferer, and then when repassing the group could not forbear remarking to them, "You see you were wrong about his *karma*." "Yes, we were wrong," they replied. "It was his *karma* to be helped by you." The same views of karma and of transmigration, as referring to the past, not the future, are apparent in a recent number of *The Inquirer*, a paper conducted in Calcutta for the benefit of Hindu students and others. I take the following from the question column: "Do Christians believe in the doctrine of reincarnation? If not, how do you account for blindness at birth?" The questioner's idea is plain, and the coincidence with the question put to Christ in St. John's Gospel, chapter ix, is striking. Hindus thus have room for an idea of the *future* of the soul, as Christians, on their side, have for a theory of the soul's origin.

The Christian idea of the Hereafter cannot, as yet, be called a strongly dynamical doctrine of Christianity in the sense that the Person of Our Lord has proved dynamical. Not that interest in the subject is lacking. I have referred to questions put by educated Hindus in *The Inquirer*. Out of fifty-seven questions I find eight bearing on the Christian doctrine of the Hereafter or the Hindu doctrine of Transmigration. In the *Magazine of the Hindu College, Benares*, out of fourteen questions I find four bearing on the same subject. The want of force in the Christian doctrine no doubt reflects its want of force for Christians themselves in this present positive age. For even Tennyson himself was vague:

"That which drew from out the boundless deep
Turns again home."

---

The new sects and the doctrine of Transmigration.

---

The *Text-book of Hindu Religion.*

---

A European's place on the ladder of transmigration.

---

Of the sects of recent origin, only the Brāhma Samāj or Theistic Association rejects the doctrine of transmigration avowedly. We have already said that the Ārya Samāj or Vedic Theists of the United Provinces and the Punjab hold strongly to the doctrine. It is noteworthy that *they* should do so, the Vedas being their standards wherewith to test Modern Hinduism, for the doctrine of transmigration is scarcely hinted at in the Vedas, and in the oldest, the Rigveda, there is said to be no trace of the doctrine.[118] It appears in the later writings, the Upanishads, and is manifest throughout the Code of Manu (c. A.D. 200). Mrs. Besant, chief figure among the Indian Theosophists, now virtually a Hindu Revival Association, preaches the doctrine, and, in fact, lectured on it in Britain in 1904. At the same time, transmigration is no part of the Theosophist's creed. As might be expected, the *Text-book of Hindu Religion*, of the Hindu College, Benares, gives the doctrine of transmigration a prominent place, although the explicitness with which it is set forth is very surprising to one acquainted with the way the doctrine is generally ignored by the educated. I quote from the *Hindu Text-book*, published in 1903, that Westerns may realise that in dealing with transmigration we are not dealing simply with some old-world doctrine deciphered from some palm-leaf written in some ancient character. After describing—here following the ancient philosophical writings, the Upanishads—how the Jivatma or Soul comes up through the various existences of the mineral, plant, and animal kingdoms until it reaches the human stage, the Text-book proceeds to describe the further upward or downward process. It is declared that the downward movement (from man to animal) is now much rarer than formerly—that concession is made to modern ideas—but the *law* of the downward process is as follows: "When a man has so degraded himself below the human level that many of his qualities can only express themselves through the form of a lower creature, he cannot, when his time for rebirth comes, pass into a human

- 120 -

form. He is delayed, therefore, and is attached to the body of one of the lower creatures as a co-tenant with the animal, vegetable, or mineral Jiva [life], until he has worn out the bonds of these non-human qualities and is fit to take birth again in the world of men. A very strong and excessive attachment to an animal may have similar results." Where modern ideas reach in India, one can understand such ideas as those melting away. A second passage from the Text-book is interesting, as showing the compiler's idea of the place of a life in Europe in the chain of existences, although in this case also the statement is made only about "ancient days." "The Jivatma [soul] was prepared for entrance into each [Indian] caste through a long preliminary stage *outside* India; then he was born into India and passed into each caste to receive its definite lessons; then was born away from India to practise these lessons; usually returning to India to the highest of them, in the final stages of his evolution." In other words, people of the outer world, say Europeans, are rewarded for virtue by being born into the lowest Indian caste, and then, after rising to be brahmans in India, they go back to Europe to give it the benefit of their acquirements; and finally crown their career by reappearing in India as a brahman philosopher or jogi. Surely we may laugh at this without being thought unsympathetic or narrow-minded. We recall Mrs. Besant's assertion that she had a dim recollection of an existence as a brahman pandit in India. According to the spiritual genealogy of the *Hindu Text-book*, she may hope to be born next in an Indian child, and become a jogi possessed of saving knowledge of the identity of self with Deity.

---

### The women of the middle class and transmigration.

---

I asked a lady who had been a missionary in Calcutta for many years, how far a belief in transmigration was apparent among the women of the middle class. She could recall only two instances in which it had come to her notice in her talks with the wives and daughters of educated India. Once a reason was given for being kind to a cat, that the speaker's grandmother might then be in it as her abode, although the observation was accompanied with a laugh. On the second occasion, when the lady was having trouble with a slow pupil, one of the women present, sympathising with the teacher, said, "Do not trouble with her; perhaps next time when she comes back she will be cleverer." The general conclusion, therefore, I repeat: Transmigration is no longer a living part of the belief of educated India; the Christian conception of the Hereafter is as yet only partially taking its place.

# CHAPTER XIX

## THE IDEAS OF SIN AND SALVATION

"Conscience does make cowards of us *all.*"

—SHAKESPEARE.

---
Recapitulation.

---

---
The new Theism.

---

In the new India, as fish out of the water die, many things cannot survive. We have seen the educated Hindu dropping polytheism, forgetting pantheism, and adopting or readopting monotheism as the basis of his religious thinking and feeling. For modern enlightenment and Indian polytheism are incongruous; there is a like incongruity between Indian pantheism and the modern demand for practical reality. Likewise, both polytheism and pantheism are inconsistent with Christian thought, which is no minor factor in the education of modern India. Further, the theism that the educated Hindu is adopting as the basis of his religion approaches to Christian Theism. The doctrines of the Fatherhood of God and the Brotherhood of Man have become commonplaces in his mouth.

---
Homage to Christ Himself

---

Likewise, the educated Hindu is strongly attracted to the person of Jesus Christ, in spite of His alien birth and His association with Great Britain. There is a sweet savour in His presence, and the man of any spirituality finds it grateful to sit at His feet. That familiar oriental expression, hyperbolical to our ears, but ever upon the lips in India to express the relationship of student to trusted professor, or of disciple to religious teacher, expresses exactly the relationship to Jesus Christ of the educated man who is possessed of any religious instinct. To such a man the miracles, the superhuman claims, the highest titles of Jesus Christ, present no difficulty until they are formulated for his subscription in some hard dogmatic mould. Then he must question and discuss.

Again, the educated Hindu finds himself employing about the dead and the hereafter not the language of transmigration, but words that convey the idea of a continuation of our present consciousness in the presence of a personal God. For life is becoming worth living, and the thought of life continuing and progressing is acceptable. This present life also has become a reality; a devotee renouncing the world may deny its reality; but how in this practical modern world can a man retain the doctrine of Maya or Delusion. It has dropped from the speech and apparently out of the mind of the educated classes.

I have suggested that those features of Christianity that are proving to be dynamical in India will be found to be those same that are proving to be dynamical in Britain. The converse also probably holds true, as our religious teachers might do well to note. The doctrines of Sin and Salvation through faith in Jesus Christ do not yet seem to have commended themselves in any measure in India. Positive repudiation of a Christian doctrine is rare, but the flourishing new sect of the North-West, the Āryas, make a point of repudiating the Christian doctrine of salvation by faith, although not explicitly denying it in their creed. Over against it they set up the Justice of God and the certainty of goodness and wickedness receiving each its meed. One can imagine that salvation by faith in Jesus Christ, the outstanding feature of Christianity, may have been unworthily presented to the Ārya leaders, so that it appeared to them merely as some cheap or gratis kind of "indulgences." The biographer of the Parsee philanthropist, Malabari, a forceful and otherwise well-informed writer, sets forth that idea of salvation by faith, or an idea closely akin. He is explaining why his religious-minded hero did not accept the religion of his missionary teachers. "The proud Asiatic," he says, "strives to purchase salvation with work, and never stoops to accept it as alms, as it necessarily would be if faith were to be his only merit." The unworthy presentation of "salvation by faith" may have occurred either in feeble Christian preaching or in anti-Christian pamphlets. Neither is unknown in India; and anti-Christian pamphlets have been known to be circulated through Ārya agencies.

To appreciate the attitude of the Hindu mind to the doctrines of Sin and Salvation, we must return again to the rough division of Hindus into—first, the mass of the people, polytheists; secondly, the educated classes, now largely monotheists; thirdly, the brahmanically educated and the ascetics, pantheists. It is only with the monotheists that we have now to deal. As already said—to the pantheist the word sin has no meaning. Where all is God, sin or alienation from God is a contradiction in terms. The conception of sin implies the *two* conceptions of God and Man, or at least of Law and Man; and where one or other of these two conceptions is lacking, the conception of sin cannot arise. In pantheism, the idea of man as a distinct individual is relegated to the region of Maya or Delusion; there cannot therefore be a real sinner. Does such reasoning appear mere dialectics without practical application, or is it unfair, think you, thus to bind a person down to the logical deductions from his creed? On the contrary, persons denying that we can sin are easy to find. Writes the latest British apostle of Hinduism, for the leaders of reaction in India are a few English and Americans: "There is no longer a vague horrible something called sin: This has given place to a clearly defined state of ignorance or blindness of the will."[119] I quote again also from Swami Vivekananda, representative of Hinduism in the Parliament of Religions at Chicago in 1893. It is from his lecture published in 1896, entitled *The Real and the Apparent Man*. His statement is unambiguous. "It is the greatest of all lies," he says, "that we are mere men; we are the God of the Universe.... The worst lie that you ever told yourself is that you were born a sinner.... The wicked see this universe as a hell; and the partially good see it as heaven; and the perfect beings realise it as God Himself. By mistake we think that we are impure, that we are limited, that we are separate. The real man is the One Unit Existence." Such is the logical and the actual outcome of pantheism in regard to the idea of sin, and such is the standpoint of Hindu philosophy.

---

Sankarachargya, the pantheist's, confession of sins.

---

Or if further illustration be needed of the incompatibility of the ideas of pantheism and sin, listen to the striking prayer of Sankarachargya, the pantheistic Vedantist of the eighth century A.D., with whom is identified the pantheistic motto, "One only, without a second."[120] It attracts our attention because Sankarachargya is professedly confessing sins. Thus runs the prayer: "O Lord, pardon my three sins: I have in contemplation clothed in form thee who art formless; I have in praise described thee who art ineffable; and in visiting shrines I have ignored thine omnipresence."[121] Beautiful expressions indeed, confessions that finite language and definite acts are inadequate to the Infinite, nay, contradictions of the Infinite, expressions fit to be recited in prayer by any man of any creed who feels that God is a Spirit and omnipresent! But in a Christian prayer such expressions would only form a preface to confession of one's own *moral* sin; after adoration comes confession. Whether, like Sankarachargya, we think of the Deity objectively, as the formless and literally omnipresent Being, the *pure Being* which, according to Hegel, equals nothing, or whether like Swami Vivekananda we think of man and God as really one, all differentiation being a delusion within the mind—there is *no second*, neither any second to sin against nor any second to commit the sin.

---
The masses and the sense of sin.
---

---
Prescriptions for sinners.
---

For the ignorant masses, the sense of sin has been worn out by the importance attached to religious and social externals and by the artificial value of the service of a hereditary monopolist priesthood. These right, all is right in the eyes of the millions of India. When one of the multitude proposes to himself a visit to some shrine or sacred spot, no doubt the motive often is some divine dissatisfaction with himself; it is a feeling that God is not near enough where he himself lives. But what is poured into his ears? By a visit to Dwaraka, the city of Krishna's sports, he will be liberated from all his sins. By bathing in the sacred stream of the Ganges he will wash away his sins. All who die at Benares are sure to go to heaven. By repeating the Gayatri (a certain verse of the Rigveda addressed to the sun) a man is saved. "A brahman who holds the Veda in his memory is not culpable though he should destroy the three worlds"—so says the Code of Manu. The Tantras, or ritual works of modern Hinduism, abound in such prescriptions for sinners. "He who liberates a bull at the Aswamedika place of pilgrimage obtains *mukti*, that is salvation or an end of his rebirths." "All sin is destroyed by the repetition of Kali's thousand names." "The water of a guru's [religious teacher's] feet purifies from all sin." "The man who carries the guru's dust [the dust of the guru's feet] upon his head is emancipated from all sin and is [the god] Siva himself." "By a certain inhalation of the breath through the left nostril, and holding of the breath, with repetition of *yam*, the Vāyu Bija or mystical spell of wind or air, the body and its indwelling sinful self are dessicated, the breath being expelled by the right nostril."[122] And so on *ad infinitum*. Superstition, Western or Eastern, has no end of panaceas. We recall the advertisements of "Plenaria indulgenzia" on the doors of churches in South Italy. Visiting Benares, the metropolis of popular Hinduism, the conception of salvation everywhere obtruded upon one is that it is a question of sacred spots, and of due offerings and performances thereat.

---

The signification of sacrifices to the Indian masses.

---

Description of animal sacrifice.

---

What to the masses is *sacrifice* even, the word which to western ears, familiar with the term in our Scriptures, suggests acknowledgment of sin and atonement therefor? It is a mistake to regard sacrifices in India as expiatory; they are gifts to the Deities as superior powers for boons desired or received, or they are the customary homage to the powers that be, at festivals and special occasions. Animal sacrifices are distinguished from the offerings of fruits and flowers only in being limited to particular Deities and pertaining to more special occasions. An actual instance will show the place that sacrifices hold. In a letter from a village youth to his father, informing him how he had proceeded upon his arrival at Calcutta, whither he had gone for the University Matriculation Examination, he reports that he has offered a goat in sacrifice in order to ensure his success. What he probably does is this. In a bazaar near the great temple of Kalighat, near Calcutta, the greatest centre of animal sacrifices in the world, he buys a goat or kid, fetches it into the temple court and hands it over to one of the priests whom he has fee'd. The priest puts a consecrating daub of red lead upon the animal's head, utters over it some mantra or sacred Sanscrit text, sprinkles water and a few flowers upon it at the actual place of slaughter, and then delivers it over again to the offerer. Then when the turn of the offerer, whom we are watching, has come, he hands over the animal to the executioner, who fixes its neck within a forked or Y-shaped stick fixed fast in the ground. With one blow the animal's head is severed from its body. The bleeding head is carried off into the shrine to be laid before the image of the goddess, and become the temple perquisite. The decapitated body is carried off by the offerer to furnish his family with a holiday meal. With his forehead ceremonially marked with a touch of the blood lying thick upon the ground, the offerer leaves the temple, his sacrifice finished. Such is animal sacrifice; if the description recalls the slaughter-house, the actual sight is certainly sickening. Yet, far as a European now feels from worship in such a place, and thankful to Him who has abolished sacrifice once for all, there is no doubt religious gratification to those who go through what I have described. Our point is that, as Sir M. Monier Williams declares, in such an offering, "there is no idea of effacing guilt or making a vicarious offering for sin."[123]

The educated classes and the idea of sin.

The brahma monopoly of nearness to the Deity broken down.

The educated classes, breathing now a monotheistic atmosphere, although in close contact with polytheism in their homes and with pantheism in their sacred literature, have reached the platform on which the idea of sin may be experienced. A member of that class, a pantheist no longer, is in the presence of a personal God, a Moral Being, and is himself a responsible person, with the instincts of a child of that Supreme Moral Being, our Father. With his education, he knows himself to be independent of brahmanical mediation in his intercourse with that Being. As confirmation, it is noteworthy how many of the religious leaders of modern times, like Buddha of old, are other than brahman by caste. In a previous chapter the names of a number of these non-brahman leaders were given. Even the Hindu ascetics of these latter days are more numerously non-brahman than of old, for in theory only brahmans have reached the ascetical stage of religious development. Whatever the reason, the brahmanical monopoly of access to and inspiration from the Deity is no longer recognised by new-educated India.

The worship of the new sects—its significance.

In like manner, the new religious associations seem to feel themselves directly in the presence of God. Congregational worship, a feature new to Hindus, is a regular exercise in the Brāhma Samāj or Theistic Association of Bengal, the Prārthanā Samājes or Prayer Associations of Western India, and the Ārya Samāj or Vedic Theistic Association of the United Provinces and the North-West of India. When Rammohan Roy, the theistic reformer, opened his church in Calcutta in 1830, he introduced among Hindus congregational worship and united prayer, before unknown among them and confessedly borrowed from Christian worship.[124] The public worship in all these bodies is indeed not unlike many a Christian service, consisting of Prayer to God, Praise of God, and expositions of religious truth. In a small collection of hymns, "Theistic Hymns," published some years ago for the use of members of the Ārya Samāj, we find many Christian hymns expressive of this personal relationship to God. We find "My God, my Father, while I stray," and "O God, our help in ages past." Neither of these hymns, however, it must be noted, contains confession of sin. Curiously incongruous to our minds is the inclusion among these hymns of poems like "The boy stood on the burning deck," and "Tell me not in mournful numbers," and "There's a magical tie to the land of our home," etc.[125] Even among the Hindu revivalists, judged by that test of the incoming of public worship, we perceive the growth of the idea of personal relationship to God. A recent publication of that party is "*Songs for the worship of the Goddess Durga.*" One of them, we may note in passing, is the well-known hymn, "Work, for the night is coming." All such personal relationship, we again repeat, is incompatible with pantheism, and almost equally so with the popular sacerdotalism. Not without significance do the new theists of Western India call their associations the Prārthanā Samājes or Prayer Associations, and give to the buildings in which they worship the name of Prayer Halls instead of temples. Let not men say that religion and theological belief belong to separable spheres.

---

The idea of sin naturally accompanies the new monotheism.

---

Once more, the public worship and prayer attendant on the new monotheism of the new religious associations are the signs that the stage has been reached where sin will be felt and confessed. As yet, however, it cannot be said that the thought of sin is prominent. In the creeds of the Ārya Samāj and the Prārthanā Samājes, the word *sin* does not occur. What we find in the Brāhma Samāj is as follows. From the creed of the Southern India Brāhma Samāj, of date about 1883, we quote paragraph 7: "Should I through folly commit sin, I will endeavour to be atoned [*sic*] unto God by earnest repentance and reformation."[126] From the "Principles of the Sadharan [Universal or Catholic] Brāhma Samāj," set forth in the organ of the body, we quote a paragraph 8: "God rewards virtue and punishes sin, but that punishment is for our good and cannot last to eternity." From a publication by a third section of the Brāhma Samāj, the party of Keshub Chunder Sen, we quote: "Every sinner must suffer the consequences of his own sins, sooner or later, in this world or in the next; for the moral law is unchangeable and God's justice irreversible. His mercy also must have its way. As the just king, He visits the soul with *adequate agonies*, and when the sinner after being thus chastised mournfully prays, He as the merciful Father delivers and accepts him and becomes reconciled to him. Such reconciliation is the only true atonement."[127] Even in the last quoted, the expression "adequate agonies" shows its standpoint regarding salvation from sin to be salvation by repentance, and not the standpoint of St. Paul, "I live, and yet no longer I, but Christ liveth in me."

# CHAPTER XX

## THE IDEA OF SALVATION

"The slender sound
As from a distance beyond distance grew,
Coming upon me—O never harp nor horn
Was like that music as it came; and then
Stream'd thro' my cell a cold and silver beam,
And down the long beam stole the Holy Grail."

TENNYSON.

> Hinduism superseded Buddhism because it offered salvation, not
> extinction.

Salvation does mean something to every class. The huge fabric of
Brahmanism does not continue to exist without ministering to some wide-
felt need of the masses. It was in obedience to some inward demand,
however perverted, that children were cast into the Ganges at Saugor, that
human sacrifices were offered and self-tortures like hook-swinging were
endured. These have been put down by British authority, but there still
remain many austerities and bloody sacrifices and strange devices to satisfy
the clamant demand of our souls. Even may we not say that, along with
other reasons for the disappearance of Buddhism from India, some
response more satisfying to the human need must have been offered by the
rival system of Hinduism. Hinduism has deities and avatars; Buddhism had
none. Two of the most interesting spots in India, the most sacred in the
world to Buddhists, are Budh-gaya, where under the bo tree Buddha
attained to enlightenment, and Sārnāth, where he began his preaching. Yet
the worship at neither place to-day is Buddhist. At the scene of Gautama's
enlightenment, where he became Buddha or Enlightened, one of the
conventional statues of Buddha is actually marked and worshipped as
Vishnu, the Hindu deity, the Preserver in the Hindu triad. Even at that
most holy shrine of Buddhism, Hinduism has supplanted it, for popular
Hinduism offered salvation, while Buddhism offered extinction. Turning
from the masses to the philosophical ascetic—when he cuts himself off
from family life with all its variety of pleasure and interest, not to speak of

the self-torture he also sometimes inflicts, he too has some corresponding demand, some adequate motive to satisfy. His is the resolute quest for salvation of the higher, older type. But we are dealing with modern, new-educated India, and now we ask ourselves: What does the modern, new-educated Indian mean by salvation? Why does the thought of salvation by faith in Jesus Christ fail to reach his heart?

---

Three ways of salvation in Hinduism: more strictly, three stages.

---

1. Saving knowledge

---

Or now Beatific Vision.

---

The acute Indian mind, with its disposition to analyse and its tenderness towards all manifestations of religion, has noted three different paths of salvation, or more strictly three stages in the path. The last only really leads to salvation, the other two paths are tolerant recognition of the well-meaning religious efforts of those who have not attained to understanding of the true and final path of salvation. For convenience sake we may roughly designate the three ways as Saving Works, and Saving Faith, and Saving Knowledge, placing the elementary stage first. One of the Tantras or ritual scriptures of Modern Hinduism, the Mahanirvāna Tantra, thus explains the three stages in the path and their respective merits: "The knowledge that Brahma alone is true is the best expedient; meditation is the middling [= the means?]; and (2) the chanting of glories and the recitation of names is the worst; and (3) the worship of idols is the worst of the worst.[128] Of the pantheist's "saving knowledge," perhaps enough has been said. But again, it is the piercing of the veil of Maya or Delusion which hides from the soul that God is the One and the All. It is the transformation of the consciousness of "I" into that of the "One only, without a second." It is the ability to say "Aham Brahman," i.e. I am Brahma. In the Life of Dr. Wilson, the Scottish Missionary at Bombay, we read that in 1833, Dr. Wilson went with a visitor to see a celebrated jogi who was lying in the sun in the street, the nails of whose hands were grown into his cheek, and on whose head there was the nest of a bird. The visitor questioned the jogi, "How can one obtain the knowledge of God?" and the reply of the jogi was, "Do not ask me questions; you may look at me, for I am God." "Aham Brahman," very probably was his reply. That is pantheistic salvation, mukti, or deliverance from further human existences and their desires and delusions. At last the spirit is free, and the galling chains of the lusting and limited body are broken. But as pantheism is declining, such cases are growing fewer, and for the educated Hindus, now largely monotheists, the saving knowledge is rather a beatific vision of the Divine, only vouchsafed to minds intensely concentrated upon the quest and thought of God, and cut off from mundane distractions. This is the union with God which is salvation to many of the modern monotheistic Hindus.

The quest of the beatific vision still implies the dissociation of religion and active life.

An unproductive religious ideal.

What concerns us here is that in the conception of the beatific vision, we still find ourselves in a different religious world from ours—religion exoteric for the vulgar, and religion esoteric for the enlightened; religion not for living by, but for a period of retirement; a religion of spiritual self-culture, not of active sonship and brotherhood. Far be it from me to say that at this point the West may not learn as well as teach, for how much thought does the culture of the spirit receive among us? How little! However that may be, this conception of the religious life is deeply rooted in educated India. The impersonal pantheistic conception of the Deity may be passing into the theistic, and even into Christian theism; the doctrine of transmigration may be little more than the current orthodox explanation of the coming of misfortune; the doctrine of Maya or the illusory character of the phenomena of our consciousness, it may be impossible to utter in this new practical age; and Jesus Christ may be the object of the highest reverence; but still the instinctive thought of the educated Hindu is that there is a period of life for the world's work, and a later period for devotion to religion. When dissatisfaction with himself or with the world does overtake him, instinctively there occur to him thoughts of retirement from the world and concentration of his mind, thereby to reach God's presence. Very few spiritually minded Hindus past middle life pass into the Christian Church, as some do at the earlier stages of life. Under the sway of the Hindu idea of salvation, by knowledge or by intense intuition, they withdraw from active life to meditate on God, with less or more of the practice of religious exercises. Painful to contemplate the spiritual loss to the community of a conception of religion that diverts the spiritual energy away from the community, and renders it practically unproductive, except as an example. Once more we recall as typical the jogi, not going about doing good, anointed with the Holy Ghost and with power, but fixed like a plant to its own spot, and with inward-looking eyes. Time was that there were jogis and joginis (female jogis) in Europe; but even of St. Theresa, at one period of her life a typical jogini, we read that not long after her visions and supernatural visitations, she became a most energetic reformer of the convents.

> The jogi, not the brahman, is the living part of present-day Hinduism.

That quest for the beatific vision or for union with God, is the highest and the most living part of present-day Hinduism, whether monotheistic or pantheistic. Not the purohit brahman (the domestic celebrant), or the guru brahman (the professional spiritual director), conventionally spoken of as divine, but the jogi or religious seeker is the object of universal reverence. And rightly so. The reality of this aspect of Hinduism is manifest in the ease with which it overrides the idea of caste. In theory brahmans are the twice-born caste, the nearest to the Deity and to union with Him. A man of lower caste, in his upward transmigrations towards union with God or absorption into Deity, should pass through an existence as a brahman. In the chapter on Transmigration we found that the upward steps of the ladder up to the brahman caste had been clearly stated in an authoritative Hindu text-book. The word *brāhman*, the name of the highest caste, is itself in fact a synonym for Deity. But as a matter of fact, men of any caste, moved by the spirit, are found devoting themselves to the jogi life. "He who attains to God is the true brāhman," is the current maxim, attributed to the great Buddha.

> Saving Faith, or Bhakti.

> Bhakti implies a personal God.

> Bhakti a genuine feeling because it may override caste.

> Bhakti not fit to cope with caste.

This brings us to the second of the three paths of salvation, the middle portion of the upward path to the mountain top of clear, unclouded vision of the All, the One Soul. In Hindu theory, at this second stage man is still amid the clouds that cling to the mountain's breast. For easy reference I have named it *Salvation by Faith*, although the English term must not mislead. The extract from the Mahanirvāna Tantra, already quoted, describes this inferior stage as the method of "chanting of glories and recitation of names" of gods. The Sanscrit name, *Bhakti*, is rendered devotion, or fervour, or faith, or fervent love; and in spite of alien ideas associated with bhakti, bhakti is much more akin to Faith than are many of the features of Hinduism to the Christian analogues with whose names they are ticketed. For example, bhakti practically implies a personal god, not the impersonal pantheistic Brahma. Intense devotion to some personal god, generally Vishnu the preserver, under the name Hari, or either of Vishnu's chief incarnations, Ram or Krishna, is the usual manifestation of bhakti. In actual practice it displays itself in ecstatic dancing or singing, or in exclaiming the name of the god or goddess, or in self-lacerations in his or her honour. Lacerations and what we would call penances, be it remembered, are done to the honour of a Deity; they are not a discipline like the self-whipping of the Flagellants and the jumping of the Jumpers of the fourteenth and fifteenth centuries. "Bhakti," says Sir Monier Williams, "is really a kind of 'meritorious work,' and not equivalent to 'faith' in the Christian sense."[129] Bhakti is the religion of many millions of India, combined more or less with the conventional externals of sacrifice and offerings and pilgrimages and employment of brahmans, which together constitute the third path of salvation, by karma or works. That ecstatic adoration is religion for many millions of India, although the name *bhakti* may never pass their lips. We judged the idea of salvation by knowledge, or by intense concentration of mind, to be *genuinely* felt, because it could override the idea of caste. Applying the same test here, we must acknowledge the genuineness of feeling in bhakti. Theoretically, at least, as Sir Monier Williams says, "devotion to Vishnu supersedes all distinctions of caste"; and again, "Vishnavism [Vishnuism], notwithstanding the gross polytheistic superstitions and hideous idolatry to which it gives rise, is the only Hindu system worthy of being called a religion."[130] In actual practice the repudiation of caste no doubt varies greatly. In some cases, caste is dropped only during the fit of fervour or bhakti. At Puri, *during* the celebrated Juggernath (Jagan-nath, Lord of the world) pilgrimage, high caste and low together receive and eat the temple food, afterwards resuming their several ranks in caste. As a matter of fact it was found at the census of 1901, that with the exception of a few communities of devotees, all the professed Vishnuites returned themselves by their caste names. Hindu bhakti, like Christianity, is in conflict with caste, and bhakti has not proved fit to cope with it.

Bhakti in other religions.

In Christian worship.

Bhakti, then, is simply the designation for fervour in worship or in presence of the Deity, as it appears in Hinduism. For fervour is not peculiar to any religion, even ecstatic fervour. We see it among the Jews in King David's dancing before the ark of the Lord, and we see it in the whirling of the dervishes of Cairo, despite Mahomedans' overawing idea of God. May we not say that the singing in Christian worship recognises the same religious instinct, and the necessity to permit the exercise of it. Many of the psalms, we feel we must chant or sing; reading is too cold for them—the 148th Psalm for example, "Praise ye the Lord from the heavens; praise Him in the heights: praise ye Him, sun and moon," and so on.

---

Bhakti a natural channel for religious feeling, now being reconsecrated.

---

We pass over the extravagances and gross depths to which bhakti, devotion or faith or love, may degenerate in the excitement of religious festivals—*corruptio optimi pessimum*. Even, strange to say, we find the grossness of bhakti also deliberately embodied in figures of wood and stone. Passing that over, we repeat that in bhakti or devotion to a personal God, or even only ecstatic extravagant devotion to a saint or religious hero semi-deified, we have a natural channel for the religious feeling of Indians, a channel that in these days is wearing deep. I speak of the middle classes, not of the ignorant masses, and my point is that the middle classes and the new religious organisations including the Indian Church are reconsecrating bhakti. Here is a portion of a bhakti hymn of one of the sections of the Brāhma Samāj:

"The gods dance, chanting the name of Hari;
Dances my Gouranga in the midst of the choral band;
The eyes full of tears, Oh! how beautiful!
Jesus dances, Paul dances, dances Sakya Muni."

---

Bhakti in the Indian Church.

---

Between singing the song and acting it while singing, the distance in India is little. The explanation of a recent Hindu devotee, Ramkrishna Paramhansa, is: "A true devotee, who has drunk deep of divine Love, is like a veritable drunkard, and as such cannot always observe the rules of propriety."[131] Manifestations of bhakti we would soon have in the Indian Christian Church were the cold moderating influence of Westerns lessened; and as the Church increases and becomes indigenous, we must welcome bhakti in measure. Every religious procession will lead to manifestations of bhakti. In the Church of Scotland Magazine, *Life and Work*, for November 1904, we are told of a convert at Calcutta: "She kept speaking and singing of Jesus.... She appeared to the Hindu family to be a Christ-intoxicated woman." Again, in the *Indian Standard* for October 1905, we read of a religious revival among the Christians of the hills in Assam, where the Welsh missionaries work. We may contrast the concomitants of the revival with those attending the late revival even among the fervid Welsh. At one meeting, we are told, "the fervour rose at times to boiling heat, and scores of men were almost beside themselves with spiritual ecstasy. We never witnessed such scenes; scores of people literally danced, while large numbers who did not dance waved their arms in the air, keeping time, as they sang some of our magnificent Khassie hymns."

Saving knowledge naturally superseded by Bhakti in the new monotheism.

An object of bhakti needed for educated India.

Buddha, Krishna, Chaitanya.

Jesus Christ, the supereminent object of bhakti.

If what I have frequently repeated in these chapters be correct—that in the nineteenth century educated India has become largely monotheistic, it is in keeping therewith that the prevailing conception of religion should have changed, alongside, from the quest of Saving Knowledge to that of Bhakti or enthusiastic devotion to a person. Direct confirmation of that inference, a recent Hindu historian supplies. In a different context altogether, he declares: "The doctrine of bhakti (Faith) now rules the Hindu to the almost utter exclusion of the higher and more intellectual doctrine of gnan (Knowledge of the Supreme Soul)." The conception of the all-comprehending impersonal Brahma has, indeed, lost vitality; for the educated also the externals of the popular religion have lost their significance and become puerile. But for them also, the objects of popular bhakti, Ram and Krishna, are as much epical as religious heroes. Hinduism needs an object of bhakti for her educated people. The fact explains several of the novel religious features of the past half-century. The great jogi, Buddha, although not a brahman, was rediscovered as a religious hero for Hindus; at the commencement of the century he was a heretic to the brahmans. "The head of a sect inimical to Hinduism," the great Rammohan Roy calls him. So Sir Edwin Arnold's *Light of Asia* had a great vogue some twenty years ago. Then Krishna has had his life re-written and his cult revived—purged of the old excesses of the Krishna-bhakti. More recently, Chaitanya, the religious teacher in Bengal in the fifteenth century, has been adopted by certain of the educated class in Bengal as an object of bhakti. Here, it seems to me, is found the place of Christ in the mind of educated India. They are fairly familiar now with the story of the New Testament, and Jesus Christ stands before them as the supereminent object of bhakti; and I venture to say is generally regarded as such, although comparatively few as yet have adopted the bhakti attitude towards Him. The *Imitatio Christi*, however, is a well-known book to the spiritually minded among the educated classes. India has advanced beyond the cold, intellectual, Unitarian appreciation of Jesus Christ that marked the early Brāhma and Prārthanā Samāj movements and manifested itself in their creeds in express denial of any incarnation. For Brāhma worship, I have seen the hymn, "Jesus, lover of my soul," transformed into "Father, lover of my soul." Hindus of the newer bhakti attitude to Christ would find no difficulty in singing the hymn as Christians do, provided the doctrinal background be not obtruded upon them. Sober faith has dawned, and will formulate itself by and by.

# CHAPTER XXI

## CONCLUSION

"Draw the curtain close,
And let us all to meditation."

SHAKESPEARE, *Hen. VI.* II.


Sailing, say to India, from Britain down through the Atlantic, close by the coast of Portugal and Spain, and then, within the Mediterranean, skirting the coast of Algeria, and so on, one is often oppressed with a sense of his isolation. We can see that the land we are passing is inhabited by human beings like ourselves; and those houses visible are homes; and signs of life we can see even from our passing vessel. What of all the tragedies and comedies that are daily being enacted in these houses—the exits and the entrances, the friendships and the feuds, the selfishnesses and self-sacrifices, the commonplace toil, the children's play, that are going on the very moment we are looking? We are out of it, and our affections refuse to be wholly alienated from these fellow-beings, although the ship of which we form a part must pursue her own aim, and hurries along.

The Briton's tie to India and Indians is of no passing accidental character. Our life-histories are not merely running parallel; our destinies are linked together. Christian feeling, duty, self-interest, and the interest of a linked destiny all call upon us to know each other and cherish mutual sympathy. Not that the West has ever been without an interest in India, as far back as we have Indian history, in the Greek accounts of the invasion of India by Alexander the Great in 327 B.C. Writing in the first century B.C. and rehearsing what the earlier Greek writers had said about India, Strabo, the Greek geographer, testifies to the prevailing interest in India, and even sets forth the difficulty of knowing India, exactly as a modern student of India often feels inclined to do. "We must take with discrimination," he says, "what we are told about India, for it is the most distant of lands, and few of our nation have seen it. Those, moreover, who have seen it, have seen only a part, and most of what they say is no more than hearsay. Even what they saw, they became acquainted with only while passing through the country with an army, in great haste. Yea, even their reports about the same things are not the same, although they write as if they had examined the things with the greatest care and attention. Some of the writers were fellow-

soldiers and fellow-travellers, yet oft-times they contradict each other....
Nor do those who at present make voyages thither afford any precise
information." We sympathise with Strabo, as our own readers also may.
The interest of the West was of course interrupted when the Turks thrust
themselves in between Europe and India and blocked the road Eastward
overland. But the sea-road round the Cape of Good Hope was discovered,
and West and East met more directly again, and Britain's special interest in
India began. Judged by the recent output of English books on India, the
interest of Britons in things Indian is rapidly increasing, and, *pace* Strabo, it
is hoped that this book, the record of the birth of New Ideas in India, will
not only increase the knowledge but also deepen interest and sympathy. For
even more noteworthy than the number of new books—since many of the
new books deal only with what may be called Pictorial India—is the
deepening of interest manifest in recent years.

That self-glorifying expression, "the brightest jewel in the British crown,"
has grown obsolete, and India has become not the glory of Britain, but the
first of her imperial responsibilities. The thought of Britain as well as the
thought of new India has changed. To the extent of recognising a great
imperial responsibility, the mission efforts of the Churches and the
speeches of statesmen and the output of the press have converted Britain.
India, what her people actually are in thought and feeling, what the country
is in respect of the necessities of life and industrial possibilities—these are
questions that never fail to interest an intelligent British audience. In this
volume, the aim has been to set forth the existing thoughts and feelings,
especially of new-educated India, and to do so on the historical principle,
that to know how a thing *has come to be*, is the right way to know what it is
and how to treat it. The history of an opinion is its true exposition. These
chapters are not speculations, but a setting forth of the progress of opinion
in India during the British period, and particularly during the nineteenth
century. The successive chapters make clear how wonderful has been the
progress of India during the century in social, political, and religious ideas.
The darkness of the night has been forgotten, and will hardly be believed
by the new Indians of to-day; and ordinary Britons can hardly be expected
to know Indian history beyond outstanding political events. Not, however,
to boast of progress, but to encourage educated Indians to further progress,
and to enlighten Britons regarding the India which they are creating, is the
hope of this volume. Further progress has yet to be made, and difficult
problems yet await solution, and to know the history of the perplexing
situation will surely be most helpful as a guide. What future is in store for
India lies hidden. It would be interesting to speculate, and with a few *ifs*
interposed, it might be easy to dogmatise. What will she become? is indeed
a question of fascinating interest, when we ask it of a child of the
household, or when we ask it of a great people rejuvenated, to whom the

British nation stands in place of parent. In the history of the soul of a people, the century just ended may be but a brief space on which to stand to take stock of what is past and seek inspiration for the future, to talk of progress made and progress possible.

"Where lies the land to which the ship would go?
Far, far ahead, is all her seamen know.
And where the land she travels from away?
Far, far behind, is all that they can say."[132]

But the past century is all the experience of India we Britons have, and we are bound to reflect well upon it in our outlook ahead.

# Footnotes

[1] The Senate and People of Rome—Senatus Populus-que Romanus.

[2] In the Hindu College at Benares, affiliated to Allahabad University, certain orthodox Hindus also objected to sacred texts being read in the presence of European professors and teachers. Think of it, in that college preparing students for ordinary modern degrees!—Bose, *Hindu Civilisation*, I. xxxiii.

[3] One of the Zoroastrian Persians who fled to Western India at the beginning of the eighth century A.D. At the census of 1901 they numbered 94,190. They are most numerous in the city of Bombay.

[4] *Asiatic Studies*, I.

[5] *Ibid.*, I. iii.

[6] *Quinquen, Report on Education in India*, 1897-1902.

[7] For an apparently contrary view, see *Census of India, 1901, Report*, p. 430: "Railways, which are sometimes represented as a solvent of caste prejudices, have in fact enormously extended the area within which those prejudices reign supreme." The sentence refers to the influence of the fashion of the higher castes in regard to child marriage and prohibition of the marriage of widows.

[8] Sir W.W. Hunter, *England's Work in India*.

[9] The manifold origins of castes are fully discussed in the newest lights in the *Census of India Report*, 1901.

[10] Miss Noble [Sister Nivedita], finds herein an apology for caste. "The power of the individual to advance is by this means kept strictly in ratio to the thinking of the society in which he lives." *(The Web of Indian Life*, p. 145.)

[11] Sir A. Lyall, *Asiatic Studies*, I. v.: "A man is not a Hindu because he inhabits India or belongs to any particular race or state, but because he is a Brahmanist." Similarly *Census of India*, 1901, *Report*, p. 360: "The most obvious characteristics of the ordinary Hindu are his acceptance of the Brahmanical supremacy and of the caste system."

[12] *Harvest Field*, March 1904; *Madras Decen. Missionary Conference Report*, 1902.

[13] Introduction to *Translation of the Ishopanishad*.

[14] *Benares Hindu Coll. Maga.* Sept. 1904.

[15] *Karkarin: Forty years of Progress and Reform*, p. 117.

[16] *Census of India*, 1901, *Report*, pp. 496, 517, 544.

[17] Miss Noble [Sister Nivedita], *Web of Indian Life*, p. 133.

[18] *Report, Census of India*, 1901, p. 163.

[19] *Census of India*, 1901, *Report*, p. 163.

[20] *Census of India*, 1901, *Report*, p. 522.

[21] *Lux Christi*, by C.A. Mason, p. 255. 1902.

[22] In Italy, in 1891, the sexes were almost equal, being males 1000 to females 995.

[23] *Census of India*, 1901, *Report*, p. 115.

[24] A case of Suttee is reported in the *Bengal Police Report* for 1903.

[25] *Report, Census of India*, 1901, pp. 442, 443.

[26] Justice Amir Ali, *Life and Teaching of Mohammed.*

[27] Sister Nivedita, *Web of Indian Life*, p. 80.

[28] *Church of Scotland Mission Record*, 1894; *East and West*, July 1905.

[29] Trotter, *India under Queen Victoria.*

[30] P. 428.

[31] *Hindu* was originally a geographical term referring to the country of the River Indus. It is derived from the Sanscrit (*Sindhu*), meaning *river*, from which also come *Indus, Sindh, Hindu, Hindi,* and *India.* The names *Indus* and *India* are English words got from Greek; they are not Indian, terms at all, although they are coming into use among educated Indians.

[32] *Hindi* is also used as a comprehensive term for all the kindred dialects of Hindustan. See R.N. Cust, LL.D, *Oecumenical List of Translations of the Holy Scriptures*, 1901. The above account follows that given in the *Census Report* for 1901.

[33] The correct form, *brahman*, not *brahmin*, is employed by the majority of recent writers.

[34] Quoted in *Census of India*, 1881.

[35] *The Web of Indian Life*, pp. 101, 298.

[36] I. xvi.

[37] *Ancient Geography of Asia*, by Nibaran Chandra Das.

[38] For other testimony to the new national feeling, see *Decen. Missionary Conference Report*, 1902, p. 305, etc.; Sister Nivedita, *Web of Indian Life*.

[39] This may not be so in the extreme south-west, where there have been Christians since the sixth century.

[40] *The Indian National Congress*, by John Murdoch, LL.D., 1898. (Christian Literature Society, Madras.)

[41] *Karkaria: Forty Years of Progress and Reform*, 1896, p. 94.

[42] *The Indian National Congress*, by John Murdoch, LL.D., p. 95. (Madras Christian Literature Society.)

[43] *The Indian National Congress*, by John Murdoch, LL.D. (Madras Christian Literature Society), p. 142, etc.

[44] *Asiatic Studies*, I. iii., II. i.

[45] *The Indian National Congress*, by John Murdoch, LL.D., p. 153. (Madras Christian Literature Society.)

[46] Smith, *Life of Alexander Duff*, 1881, Chapter V.

[47] *Asiatic Studies*, II. I. 7, 37.

[48] *Report of Madras Decennial Missionary Conf.*, 1902, p. 311.

[49] Acts iv. 33.

[50] Acts xvii. 18, 32.

[51] *Statistical Atlas of India*, 1895.

[52] Census of 1901.

[53] *Hinduism and its Modern Exponents*, by Rev. C.N. Banerji, B.A.

[54] Monier Williams, *Brahmanism*, etc., p. 18.

[55] Monier Williams, *Hinduism*, p. 38.

[56] Youngson, *Punjab Mission of the Church of Scotland*, p. 27.

[57] "The Arya Samaj," by Rev. H.D. Griswold, D.D., *Madras Decen. Mission. Conference Report*; "The Arya Samaj," by Rev. H. Forman, *Allahabad Mission Press*, 1902; *Biographical Essays*, by Max Müller—"Dyananda Saraswati"

[58] For another explanation of the separation, see Lillie, *Madame Blavatsky*, chap. vii.

[59] 62,458,077 Mahomedans at Census of 1901.

[60] *Census of India*, 1901, *Report*, pp. 371-73.

[61] Disguised as *Necharis* in the *Report, Census of India*, 1901, p. 373. See Youngson, *Punjab Mission of the Church of Scotland*, p. 14; *Madras Decen. Miss. Conf. Report of* 1902, p. 341.

[62] *Asiatic Studies*, I. 1.

[63] Guru-prasad Sen in *Introduction to the Study of Hinduism*, quoted in *Madras Decen. Miss. Conf. Report*, p. 280.

[64] Sister Nivedita, *Web of Indian Life*, pp. 175, 179.

[65] Cf. *Philosophic Hinduism*, p. 27, Madras, C.V.E.S.

[66] Amy W. Carmichael, *Things as they are in South India*.

[67] Monier Williams, *Brahmanism and Hinduism*, p. 54.

[68] *Indian Missions from the Outside*.

[69] *Hinduism*, p. 88. *Things as They Are*, iv. by Amy W. Carmichael.

[70] *Intellectual Progress of India*, P. Mitter, p. 5.

[71] *Defence of Hindu Theism: Appeal to the Christian Public* (II. 91).

[72] Smith, *Life of Dr. Wilson*.

[73] Rammohan Roy, *Appeal to the Christian Public*.

[74] *Vedic Hinduism*, (Madras C.V.E.S.) 1888.

[75] Bose, *Hindu Civilisation during British Rule*, i. 95.

[76] Monier Williams, *Modern India*, 1878, p. 101.

[77] Plato in the *Timæus* teaches the eternal existence of matter as a substance distinct from God. See also p. 134.

[78] Max Müller, *Ramakrishna*, p. 48.

[79] Sister Nivedita, *The Web of Indian Life*.

[80] Monier Williams, *Brahmanism and Hinduism*, p. 25, etc.

[81] For the Yoga System, see pp. 127, 128, 134.

[82] *Text-book of Hindu Religion*, etc., p. 60.

[83] See *also Life of Rev. J.J. Weitbrecht*, 1830, p. 318.

[84] Max Müller, *Ramakrishna*, p. 8.

[85] *Weekly Statesman* (Calcutta), 14 IX. 1905.

[86] Rev. Dr. Griswold in *Madras Decen. Missionary Conf. Report*, 1902, p. 317.

[87] *Asiatic Studies*, II. i. 11.

[88] Sister Nivedita, *The Web of Indian Life*, pp. 191, 287.

[89] Avatar=a descent.

[90] Lillie, *India and its Problems*.

[91] Smith, *Life of Dr. John Wilson*, pp. 63, 65.

[92] Lillie, *India and its Problems*, p. 130.

[93] *Biographical Sketch of K.M. Banerjea*, p. 79. K.M. Banerjea, *Christianity and Hinduism*, pp. 1, 2, 11. Monier Williams, *Hinduism*, p. 36, etc; *Brahmanism and Hinduism*, pp. 4, 14, 17, 33. Compare Hebrews i. 2, 3.

[94] *Hinduism and its Modern Exponents*, Rev. C.N. Banerjea, B.A. Calcutta, 1893.

[95] *Sketches of Indian Christians* (Madras C.L.S.), 1896.

[96] *Lectures in India*.

[97] P.N. Mitter, *Intellectual Progress of Modern India*.

[98] *U.F. Church of Scot. Mission Report* for 1903; *Madras Decen. Missionary Conference Report*, 1903, pp. 310, 311.

[99] Farquhar, *The Future of Christianity in India* (Chr. Lit. Soc).

[100] K.C. Banurji, Esq., M.A., B.L., Registrar of Calcutta University.

[101] *Asiatic Studies*, I. v. 143.

[102] *Madras Decen. Miss. Conf. Report*, 1902, p. 345.

[103] Translated by Rev. J.L. Thakur Das, of Lahore.

[104] J.N. Farquhar, M.A., in *The Future of Christianity in India*, Madras C.L.S.

[105] For a fuller statement, see Farquhar, *The Future of Christianity in India*. C.L.S., Madras.

[106] Flint, *Philosophy of History*.

[107] *Asiatic Studies*, I. i.

[108] Bhag. Gita, v. 3, quoted by Max Müller in *Ramakrishna*, p. 3.

[109] *Asiatic Studies*, II. i. 35.

[110] John v. 11.

[111] The term *Nirvana* is not used by ordinary uneducated Indians: it is known only to the educated.

[112] Max Müller, *Ramakrishna.*

[113] Sister Nivedita, *The Web of Indian Life.*

[114] Rev. H. Forman, *The Arya Sarmāj*, Allahabad.

[115] *Madras Decen. Missionary Conf. Report*, 1902, p. 276.

[116] Hastie, *Hindu Idolatry and English Enlightenment.*

[117] "The tendency of the doctrine of Karma has been to promote contentment."—Bose, *Hindu Civilisation*, I. lix.

[118] Sir M. Monier Williams' *Brahmanism and Hinduism.*

[119] Sister Nivedita, *The Web of Indian Life*, p. 198.

[120] Taken from the Chhāndogya Upanishad.

[121] Lilly, *India and its Problems.*

[122] K.S. Macdonald, *Sin and Salvation ... in the Tantras*, Calcutta Methodist Publ. House.

[123] *Brahmanism and Hinduism*, pp. 25, 24; *Hinduism*, p. 39.

[124] Monier Williams, *Brahmanism and Hinduism.*

[125] *The Ārya Samā[=i]*, by Rev. Henry Forman. Allahabad, 1887.

[126] *Religious Reform*, Part IV. Madras C.V.E.S., 1888.

[127] *Religious Reform*, Part IV. Madras C.V.E.S., 1888.

[128] K.S. Macdonald, *Sin and Salvation ... in the Tantras.* Calcutta Methodist Publ. House.

[129] Monier Williams, *Brahmanism and Hinduism*, p. 63.

[130] Monier Williams, *Brahmanism and Hinduism*, Chap. V.

[131] Max Müller, *Ranuikrishna Paramahansa*, p. viii.

[132] A.H. Clough. Quoted by Lord Curzon at Simla, September 1905.